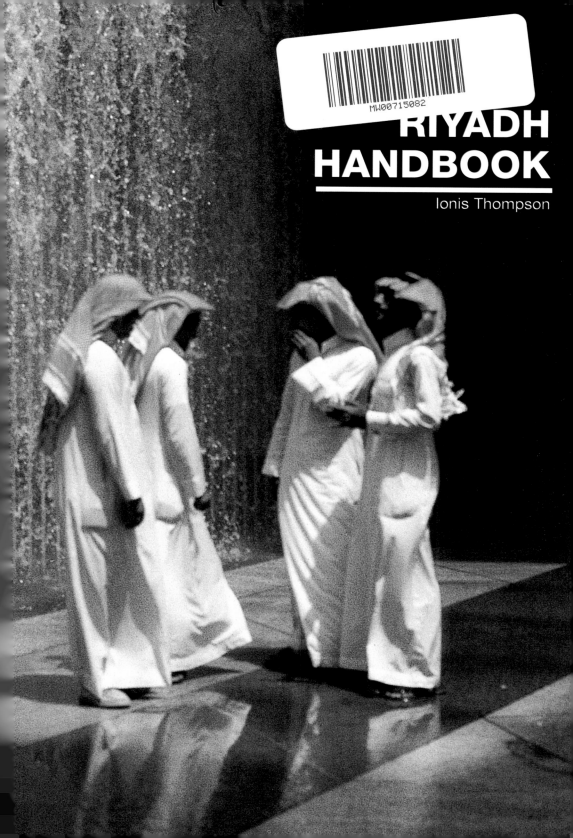

MW00715082

RIYADH
HANDBOOK

Ionis Thompson

Riyadh Handbook
Ionis Thompson
updated by Lisa Greenberg

© Stacey International 2000

First edition 1996

ISBN: 0 900988 223

All rights reserved. No part of this
publication may be reproduced,
stored in a retrieval system, or
transmitted in any form or by any
means, electronic, mechanical, photographic or otherwise, without prior
permission of the copyright owner.

Designed by Kitty Carruthers
Printed in Bahrain by Oriental Press

PICTURE CREDITS: All pictures by Ionis Thompson,
with the exception of the following:
Cover & p 67: Martyn Best;
half title page: John Herbert;
pp:7, 14, 17, 26, 41, 62, 67, 71, 75(2), 77, 78: Lisa
Greenberg. Thanks are due also to the *Riyadh Daily* for
help in picture research.

British Library Cataloguing-in-Publication Data
A catalogue record for this book is available from the
British Library.

No guide can claim to be wholly
comprehensive. This is a personal
selection of the services and
products available in Riyadh,
checked, sampled and endorsed as
far as possible by the author, who
has no commercial interest in any of
the companies mentioned. The
information is as up-to-date as
possible at the time of going to
press. Where a (T) appears in the
text, the telephone number is shown
in the margin. A full list of telephone numbers can be found at the
end of the book.

Riyadh Handbook

IONIS THOMPSON

updated by
LISA GREENBERG

STACEY INTERNATIONAL

Contents

BEFORE YOU GO: A FEW
HELPFUL FACTS   6

A Brief History of Riyadh   **6**
The Country   **7**
  Climate   7
  Health   8
  Calendar   8
  Time   9
  Currency and Banking   9
  News and Broadcasting   9
  Driving   10
The People   **10**
The Documents You Need   **13**
  Visas   13
What to Take   **14**
  Food   14
  Medicine   14
  Books   14
  Music   15
  Clothes   15
  Things for the Home   15
  Sports   16
  Electrical Equipment   16

LIVING IN RIYADH   **17**

Housing   **17**
  Where to Live   17
  Security   18

  Maintenance   18
  Pest Control   19
  Utilities   19
  Water   19
  Domestic Help   20
Medical   **20**
  Hospitals   20
  Clinics   21
  Dental Services   22
  Optical Services   23
  Mental Health   23
  Veterinary Services   23
  Emergencies   23
  Pharmacies   23
  Health Hazards   24
Opportunities for Women   **24**
Opportunities for Men   **26**
Postal Services and
  Telephones   **26**
  Internet and e-mail   28
Shopping   **28**
  Opening Times   28
  Department Stores   29
  Supermarkets   30
  Shopping Centres   31
  Suqs   32
  Auctions   35
  Shopping by Product   35
Services   **48**
  Barbers and Hairdressers 48

Catering	48
Dry-cleaners	49
Movers and Packers	49
Painting and Decorating	49
Printers	49
Tailors, Dressmakers and Handicrafts	49
Upholstery and Furnishings	50
Transport and Travel	**50**
Travel Letters	50
Buses	50
Taxis	51
Driving Licence	51
Buying a Car	52
Spare Parts	53
Car Hire	53
Driving Manners and Customs	53
Accidents	54
Train Travel	54
Coaches	54
Air Travel	54
Hotels and Restaurants	**55**
Hotels	55
Restaurants	56
Libraries	**58**
Banks	60
Education	**61**
Nursery	61
Primary and Secondary	61
Adult Education	62

THINGS TO DO AND SEE AROUND RIYADH	**65**
The Desert	**65**
Sightseeing and Spectator Sports	**65**
Dira Square	65
Musmak Fortress	65
King Abdulaziz National Historical Centre	66
Murabba Palace	66
Dir'iyyah	68
Janadriyah & Camel Races	69
Horse Races	70
Natural History and Science	**70**
The Zoo	70
The Science Oasis	70
NCWCD Visitor Centre	71
King Khalid Wildlife Research Centre	72
King Faisal Centre for Research and Islamic Studies	72
Parks	**73**
Sports	**74**
Private Sports	75
Public Sports and Clubs	75
Golf	76
Football	76
Activities for Children	**76**
Organised Tours in Riyadh	**79**
Telephone Numbers	**80**
Additional Reading	**88**
Maps	**89**

BEFORE YOU GO: A FEW HELPFUL FACTS

A Brief History of Riyadh

Riyadh, capital of Saudi Arabia, lies on the great limestone plateau of Nejd, in the centre of the Arabian peninsula, some 2500 feet above sea level. Its name means 'gardens' or silt beds; it lies on a silt plain surrounded by palm groves, near the fertile bed of the Wadi Hanifah. This great watercourse linked the towns which lay along its bed with the east coast, and so Riyadh served as a trade centre on the pilgrim route across the peninsula. We know from early Arabic sources that a settlement existed on this site before the fifth century AD and that it continued to flourish over the succeeding centuries, first under the protection of the Umayyads of Damascus, later of the Abbasids of Baghdad and then of the amirs of al-Hasa. The first settlement on the site was known as Hajar, and the name was changed to Riyadh in the twelfth century. In the seventeenth century the town was enclosed with walls, which were destroyed by the Rashids when they occupied the town in the nineteenth century. King Abdulaziz later rebuilt the walls, reinforcing them with towers and adding gates, all of which have also since been destroyed.

Riyadh gave way to Dir'iyyah as the chief town of the area after the latter's foundation in the fifteenth century. Dir'iyyah became the capital of the first Saudi dynasty which, under the reforming banner of the eighteenth-century Shaykh Muhammad ibn Abd al-Wahhab, succeeded in controlling much of the Arabian peninsula. This success attracted the enmity of the Ottoman Empire, and in 1818 a force was sent from Egypt under Ibrahim Pasha to destroy the power of the al-Saud. By 1821 the great city of Dir'iyyah

Dir'iyyah, the old city

Recreation of traditional well in the Historical Centre Plaza

had been all but razed to the ground and abandoned: its remains can still be seen today.

In the 1820s the seat of Saudi authority was moved to Riyadh and a period of relative peace and order followed. Control was re-established not only over Nejd but also over al-Hasa and Qasim. In 1865, however, the death of the Imam Faisal was followed by a ten-year period of civil war, which reduced Riyadh's status to that of district capital of southern Nejd. Al-Hasa fell under Ottoman control and Qasim reasserted its independence. In 1875 the al-Rashid of Hail took control of Riyadh, which continued to slumber in obscurity. The al-Saud family dispersed and Abdul Rahman, father of Abdulaziz, took refuge in Kuwait. In December 1901 the young Abdulaziz, with a small band of followers, set out from here on his daring expedition to regain control of Riyadh. He seized the Musmak fortress on January 15th 1902, killed the Rashidi governor, and restored Saudi rule over Riyadh.

From his base in Riyadh, Abdulaziz gradually established control over a vast area from the Gulf to the Red Sea, which in 1932 became the Kingdom of Saudi Arabia.

The Country

Climate
Riyadh's atmosphere is almost completely free from humidity. The winter climate is delightful, warm during the day and cool at night. Daytime temperatures range between about 6° C and 10° C in January and the mid to high 40s° C in mid-summer. Night-time temperatures are lower, dropping very sharply during the winter months. It can get colder than these averages during December, January and February, occasionally dropping below zero, and hotter during the middle of summer, especially during

June, July and August. Air-conditioning is universal and during the summer months most of the day is spent indoors, but the early mornings and evenings are balmy and delightful even during the hottest months. Temperatures are always lower in the desert. Rainy periods may occur at any time between December and April and usually last intermittently for two weeks or so.

Health
Riyadh is a healthy place to live, perhaps thanks to its dry climate, and health care is excellent. The authorities recommend immunisation against typhoid, tetanus and hepatitis A, but this is not compulsory and most people do not bother. During the Haj pilgrimage each year, the government usually recommends immunisation against meningitis and sometimes refuses entry into the Kingdom without a signed and dated statement from a physician confirming immunisation. Riyadh is not a malarial area. Due to the rapid greening and industrialisation of Riyadh, the air contains many more allergens than previously. During the cold season from October through February, the incidence of hay fever and asthma is relatively high. Those who suffer from hayfever and/or asthma would be well advised to have a good supply of medicine on hand.

Calendar
There are two calendars in use in the Kingdom, the Gregorian and the Hijra or lunar calendar, the official one, which dates from the migration (Hijra) of the Prophet Muhammad and his followers from Makkah to Medina in AD 622. There are twelve lunar months of almost equal length. A sighting of the new moon is required to mark the beginning of each month, which can result in a day's variation either way. There is a difference of about eleven days between the the Gregorian calendar and the Hijra one. This means that the Hijra year, which starts with the month of Muharram, falls eleven days earlier each year, according to western reckoning, and the months of Ramadan (the month of fasting) and Dhu al-Hijja (the month

King Abdul Aziz mosque, near the Diplomatic Quarter.

of pilgrimage, the Haj) likewise fall about eleven days earlier each year. This is relevant to the non-Muslim as well as to the Muslim, as everyone is required to observe the dictates of the fasting period, that is, to abstain from drinking, eating and smoking in public from sunrise to sunset.

At the end of Ramadan there is an Islamic holiday, the Eid al-Fitr, which lasts five days into the following month, Shawwal. Public offices are closed for about two weeks, private businesses for less. This is a time for families to get together, and a lot of visiting takes place between friends, relations and business acquaintances. About ten weeks after the end of Ramadan, on the tenth of Dhu al-Hijja, there is another Islamic holiday, the Eid al-Adha. This also lasts two weeks for public offices, less for private ones, and is an important time for families.

There are five prayer times during each day, during which shops and some businesses close (*see* page 28).

The working week in Saudi Arabia runs from Saturday to Wednesday. Government and other offices are closed all day Thursday and Friday, but most private businesses operate on a five and a half day week, closing at Thursday lunchtime.

Time

Riyadh is three hours ahead of Greenwich Mean Time. There is one time zone throughout the Kingdom, but the times of prayer will be slightly different in the regions because of the different times of sunrise and sunset. These times are given every day in the local English-language newspapers.

Currency and Banking

The currency in the Kingdom is the Saudi riyal, divided into 100 halalas. It is based on the US dollar and there are approximately SR3.75 to the $1. The exchange rates can be found daily in the English-language newspapers. Cash is often preferred, but hotels, restaurants, and the larger stores accept credit cards. Most large grocery stores accept the point of sale SPAN system; SPAN debit cards are issued by all local banks. Cheques may be used for transactions between businesses and for payment for services such as the Internet. Riyadh residents may choose from a number of different banks, with branches in most parts of the city. Banks often have ATM machines attached, some of which are drive-in services, and ATM machines are also present in locales such as supermarkets, airports, and even on street corners. Traveller's cheques can be bought in the banks.

News and Broadcasting

There are three daily English-language newspapers available; *The Riyadh Daily* published in Riyadh and the *Arab News* and the *Saudi Gazette* published in Jeddah. A variety of regional

English language business magazines, such as *Middle East Economic Digest* and *Saudi Economic Survey*, are also sold locally and are available by subscription. Some foreign newspapers and a limited selection of magazines and periodicals are imported, usually two days after their publication dates in Europe. These are all subject to censorship. You can find newspapers and magazines in every major supermarket, hotel and bookshop.

The Television Tower

Radio   The BBC Overseas Service is currently broadcast in the Middle East on these frequencies: 9410 KHz in the mornings and evenings, 11760 KHz mornings and daytime,15575 KHz all day, 11995 and 12095 KHz evenings only. Current frequencies can be determined by contacting the local British Council or the Internet site [www.bc.co.uk/world-service]. Radio Riyadh (T) broadcasts on 97.7 FM with a varied programme in English (8-11 am and 1-3:30 pm, and 7-12 pm), French (11 am-1 pm and 5-7 pm), and Urdu (3.30-5 pm). The news in French is broadcast at 12 noon and in English at 3 pm.

Radio Riyadh	403 8111

Television   Saudi Arabia operates a two-channel television system. Channel 1 is in Arabic, Channel 2 in English. The English-language news is broadcast every day at 8.30 pm and the French language news is broadcast at 7:30 pm. Two companies, Orbit (T) and al-Jazeera Showtime (T), offer satellite TV with numerous channels, including Discovery, ESPN, BBC news, CNN, and movies and cartoons. Satellite dishes can also be brought locally from companies such as Thimar (T).

Orbit	479 3464
Al-Jazeera Showtime	435 4633
Thimar	477 7690

Driving

Women are not permitted to drive in Saudi Arabia. Many compounds have a regular bus service to schools and shops. Employment contracts may include the cost of a driver – some families share the use of one.

The People

Every aspect of life in Saudi Arabia, Islam's heartland, is governed by religion and it is helpful to non-Muslims to be aware of some of the implications of this. The Kingdom is home to the two holiest places in Islam and the King is the custodian of these sites. Places of worship for other religions are excluded, as, indeed, are collective acts of worship and overtly displayed symbols of other religions, such as a cross. Other religions' festivals are not acknowledged and Christian symbolism, as for example on greeting cards, is not acceptable. Islamic symbolism excludes living things and this leads some people to object to the public use of the camera, which can be taken as an intrusion upon privacy. There is also considerable sensitivity towards the camera on security grounds, and the photographing of some public places may be discouraged.

Living in the country one soon comes to appreciate that the Holy Quran, being the word of God, is in itself an object of sanctity and should therefore be treated with the utmost respect by both Muslims and non-Muslims.

The spiritual austerity of Islam in Saudi Arabia precludes any emphasis on overt sexuality and any exposure of flesh. Stripping to the waist, for whatever purpose, is not acceptable for men and can offend, as can the wearing of shorts by either men or women. The most convenient way for women to adapt to this precept is for them to wear the thin black cloak, the *abaya*, over their normal clothes when out and about. Alternatively, a long-sleeved full-length garment will meet the requirement. The wearing of neck jewellery by men is strictly against Islamic custom.

It follows also that printed advertisements based on female allure are removed or blacked out from imported journals and newspapers, videos featuring sexual relations are not permitted, and representations of those other aspects of western life prohibited under Islam, such as the consumption of alcohol, are expunged or banned. If customs officials encounter books

Roof of the Murabba Palace

or videos with suggestive covers in the baggage of a new arrival, these items will be confiscated.

Cleanliness is one of the central injunctions of Islam, and so the feet, with their connotation of grime, and particularly the soles of the feet, are not presented to others. For a Muslim, washing is imperative before the act of prayer.

By the same token, so is absolute sobriety: in Saudi Arabia the prohibition on the use of alcohol is total. This applies to Muslims and non-Muslims alike. Dietary rules enjoined in the Holy Quran also prohibit all pork products.

Both the sanctity and the privacy of the family structure are ardently upheld. Western ways may often be taken, or mistaken, as excessively free and easy. For instance, it would be a mistake to be seen exchanging a social kiss, or holding hands, with a member of the opposite sex on the doorstep or at the airport. Travelling by car, or going out on foot, with a member of the opposite sex to whom you are not related by bonds of kinship or marriage is also to be avoided. Women out alone can attract unwanted attention, and it is therefore inadvisable for women to wander about on their own in public places, while engaging in conversation with strange men can be misinterpreted. Like all societies, Saudi Arabia is evolving. A Saudi husband and wife familiar with western ways may join a western family at table as a couple; others will prefer to entertain or be entertained separately, men with men and women with women. Until an acquaintanceship is well established, a western man would be going beyond his rights if he enquired after the wife of a Saudi friend.

A traditional welcome

Encountering Saudis socially, a westerner may acceptably address a man as Mr, followed either by the given name (e.g. Mr Khalid) or, more formally, by the family or tribal name (e.g. Mr al-Qahtani), or, in introductions, by both (e.g. Mr Khalid al-Qahtani). To drop the affix 'al' can cause offence. Some Saudis, of course, are Princes or Excellencies. Most Saudi women use their maiden names even after marriage.

If invited to a Saudi home, you may find yourself eating a traditional Saudi meal. The right hand, and the right hand only, is used to carry food to the mouth. Your host or neighbour at the meal will enthusiastically ply you with the choicest pieces. Coffee is offered at all occasions, usually Arabia's famous *gahwah*, an admirably refreshing compound of coffee and cardamom, taken in tiny handleless cups. These will be refilled repeatedly until you indicate your satisfaction by a little waggle of the empty cup, customarily after the third cup. It is not the practice in Saudi society to linger on and talk after the meal. After washing your right hand (which you will also have washed before the start of the meal), you should take your leave.

A basic rule of life in Saudi Arabia is never to be in a hurry. Negotiating is part of the fabric of life: the give and take of coming to a deal (in business, shopping or any other of life's transactions) is to be relished for its own sake. Business always commences with an exchange of pleasantries and polite enquiries – it would be a breach of etiquette to launch straight into the subject to be discussed.

The Documents You Need

Visas

As a new employee coming to work in Saudi Arabia, you will arrive in the Kingdom for the first time on a temporary visit visa arranged by your sponsor, who will be either a Saudi national or a company registered to do business in Saudi Arabia. Visas are issued for short periods, and the visit must commence within a month of the visa's date of issue. It is easy to apply for a visa too early and find it has expired before you set out! During your stay you must submit all the papers necessary to support an application for a residence visa. Among these are a medical certificate (which may have to be attested by a recognised authority) and certificates verifying your educational qualifications (which will have to be translated into Arabic.) The application takes between one month and six weeks to process, at which point the residence visa can be collected from the Saudi Embassy in your country of origin. This entitles you to apply for and receive an identity card *(iqama)*, which you must carry with you at all times. With this in your hand you may apply for your family to join you, a procedure which is unlikely to take longer than a month, and you may also apply for a driving licence (*see* page 51). Married women are entered on their husband's *iqama* as dependants, and

The Ministry of Interior

will not have one of their own, but should carry a photo-copy of their husband's *iqama* at all times. The same goes for dependant children. Single women will have their own *iqamas*.

If you wish to leave the country, for business or pleasure, you will require an exit/re-entry visa, which can be obtained for you by your sponsor. Your passport will normally be held by your sponsor and on your departure abroad will be temporarily exchanged for your *iqama*. It may be possible to acquire a multiple exit/re-entry visa, which will entitle you to make several visits over a six-month period, but these are sometimes difficult to obtain.

A single woman, or a married woman on a single *iqama*, must be met at the airport by her sponsor or his representative.

If you plan to bring a pet with you, certain restrictions apply. The Kingdom carefully controls the health of animals imported into the Kingdom. Check with your local Saudi Arabian consulate or embassy for the current rulings as restrictions change from country to country. Usually an up-to-date vaccination record and a certificate of health issued by an accredited veterinarian and stamped by the Saudi Arabian consulate or embassy are required.

What to Take

Food

There is no need to bring any foodstuffs as you will find an excellent range of food in Riyadh, including nearly everything you are used to in your home country, with the exception of a few speciality foods. Saudi Arabia now produces its own fruit and vegetables and a good variety of these now appears in the shops, including delicious summer fruit, such as grapes, melons, peaches, apricots and cherries.

Medicine

You can buy most medicines in Riyadh, many without pre-scription, but it is wise to bring anything you depend on in case it is not available.

Books

Jarir 462 6000

Riyadh has three major bookstores which stock English and French language books: Jarir (T) which sells all the recent bestsellers in English and has a good selection of travel guides and other reference books: al-Shegrey (T), and Tihama (T). A good atlas and maps of those countries which you plan to visit would be valuable additions to a personal library. If children will be attending school in Riyadh, a set of reference books or an encyclopedia on CD for school projects is critical. Many people find themselves with an unprecedented opportunity to read; if you have a particular course of reading you want to pursue, bring those books with you. Private book discussion groups meet regularly and can be found by asking on compounds or at embassies.

Tihama	401 2969
Al-Shegrey	462 8684

Music
Music tapes and cassettes and videos should also be on your list, as availability in Riyadh is limited, but remember that everything you bring into the Kingdom will be subject to censorship.

Clothes
On the whole you should bring the clothes you are used to wearing at home, with the exception of heavy winter over-coats and raincoats, which are unnecessary. Cotton, linen and silk feel more comfortable in the summer when you are moving about, but much of your time then will be spent in the comfortable cool of air-conditioned houses, when man-made fabrics are perfectly suitable. Women are required to have their arms and legs covered when out and about, and most wear the black cloak, the *abaya*, over their other clothes. Life in Riyadh involves a lot of entertaining, both formal and informal, and so a variety of casual and evening dress is needed, especially by women.

For the desert you will need sweaters, jackets, trousers in a stout material, hats to shade the face and good lace-up shoes. It is easy to find a good variety of dressmaking materials, and tailors who will copy something or follow an easy pattern at very reasonable cost (*see* pages 40 and 49). This is true for both men and women. It is also increasingly possible to find designer and off-the-peg clothes in Riyadh, and to pay no more for them than in your own country. You will also find a good choice of sports clothes and shoes (*see* page 38).

Things for the Home
Houses in Riyadh are usually quite spacious by European standards. You may find you have large areas of white wall in your reception rooms, and you will feel much more at home if you have brought with you pictures, posters and other wall coverings. It is also a good idea to bring a few other decorations and your tableware, to make your house more like a home when you first arrive. Later you will find attractive things to buy to add to these. There are plenty of shops in

IKEA   488 3233

Riyadh, such as IKEA (T), where Europeans can find familiar things for the house at reasonable prices. Most people entertain at home, so bring with you everything you use to host dinner parties. Many decorative accessories, such as candles and party items are available in Riyadh and the easiest thing of all is to have a party catered by a local hotel or restaurant.

Sports
There are plenty of opportunities to play tennis, squash, golf and other sports in Riyadh, so take your sports clothes and equipment.

Electrical Equipment
Before deciding which electrical appliances to take with you, check whether your house has both 220 and 110 voltage, as is the case in most of the older houses, or only 220, more likely if the house is new. The frequency in Riyadh is 60 AC, as in the USA, and not 50, as in Europe, which may cause problems with some of your equipment if you bring it from Europe.

LIVING IN RIYADH

Newcomers to Riyadh are urged to register with their embassies as soon as they arrive. This is to enable the embassies to make contact with their nationals in case of emergency. Through the embassies, or other national bodies, such as the American Community Services (ACS), you can also find out what is going on in Riyadh, in addition to those activities described below.

All residents must carry an identity card (*iqama*), with a photograph of the holder. In the case of a man whose residence permit allows him to be accompanied by his wife, a photocopy of the *iqama* must be made for his wife to carry, with her photograph and those of any dependant children.

Visitors must always carry their passport, and it is a good rule of thumb to memorise your embassy telephone number (*see* page 86).

A Saudi family home.

A copy of the Farsi Maps book, *Riyadh A to Z,* available at local bookstores, will help you orient yourself to Riyadh quickly. While personal and limo drivers often have a knowledge of city landmarks, they may not know exactly where your friends and business acquaintainces live and work. *Riyadh A to Z* will help you get where you want to go with a minimum of stress.

Housing

Where to Live
As Riyadh has spread north, north-east and east, so also have the living areas favoured by expatriates for their villas and compounds. Sulaimaniya and Olaya are popular, particularly for individual villas, but many of the large compounds are situated much further out. There are several near the British School, for

example, by exit 9 of the Ring Road. (A list of the telephone numbers of the main compounds is given at the back of this book).

Most expatriates live in compounds provided by their companies. There are a number of private villas for rent, many with small gardens or sitting-out areas, and either an individual swimming pool or part-share in a communal one. When choosing a residence, consider these questions: Is the location convenient to schools, shopping, restaurants, activities that you use? What transportation, recreational, and dining facilities are available in the area or from the compound? What mix of residents lives on the compound or in the neighbourhood? Do you want to live in the city center or on the outskirts? Before making a decision, ascertain all the costs involved; some rentals are quoted inclusive of all services and maintenance and others are not.

There are estate agents, or real estate offices, all over Riyadh, which will help you locate a house. A reliable one is Creators (T), in Thalateen Olaya Street (not far from the old airport), which covers most residential areas, including Sulaimaniya, Olaya, Worood, Salahadin, King Fahad Quarter, Malaaz, Rawda and Rabwa. Al-Ola Real Estate (T), in Aruba Road, and al-Bakar Real Estate (T), in Thalateen Olaya Street, cover most of these areas but not Rabwa and Rawda.

Creators	478 6708
Al-Ola Real Estate	465 9704
Al-Bakar Real Estate	465 5006

Security
House-breaking is rare in Riyadh but can occur. If you find yourself the victim of burglary or theft, you should report it immediately to the police, by ringing 999. You will need to be able to give concise verbal directions to your house, and it may be a good idea to do this with the help of an Arabic speaker. Strong locks should secure every door and window, and the car should be kept locked. If you go away for a long period, as many do here in the summer, it is a good idea to leave someone in your house to keep an eye on it. Don't neglect the precautions normal in any country.

Maintenance
When you take on the lease of a property, which will normally be for one year, check that the maintenance is included or that your company will pay for this work, as otherwise you can be involved in a lot of expense. There are companies specialising in villa maintenance, including electrical, plumbing and carpentry work, for example Electrolux Saudi Services Company Ltd (T), which will also undertake cleaning, decoration and the repair of furniture and house interiors. Creators Maintenance Service (T) also offers a full maintenance service for houses, while Bin Gaith Establishment for Air Conditioning (T) handles air conditioning.

There are specialist companies which look after swimming-pools and sell the necessary equipment and maintenance

Electrolux	419 2106
Creators Maint. Service	477 5863
Bin Gaith Est.	465 5247

products (such as costly chlorine). One such is Desert
Swimming Pools (T), on Thalateen Sulaimaniya Street.
    A useful source for the sale and repair of vacuum cleaners
is Elmark (T), on Mursalaat.

Desert Swimming Pools	463 1696
Elmark	465 1581
SAMES	476 9998
Obal	463 4476

Pest Control
It is wise to take out a contract for periodic visits to check for
rats, cockroaches and other pests. Among companies offering
this service are SAMES Pest Control (T) and Obal (T).

Utilities
Try to find a villa which already has a telephone installed, in
order to save time and trouble. Electricity and water bills are
delivered to your electricity meter box, which should therefore
be checked regularly. The telephone bill is sent by post to the
owner of the phone (i.e. your landlord), and will be itemised by
country and number called, the duration of the call and its cost
– a most useful service, but given in Arabic only. Pay your
electricity, phone and water bills promptly or the services may
be cut off! Payment is made by taking the signed bill to your
bank branch where it can be debited against your account or,
if you wish to pay by cash, taking the bill to any bank branch.
Alternatively someone acting on your behalf, such as your driver, can do this for you. Telephone bills can also be paid at
designated telephone offices, such as the one at the intersection of Khorais and Ring Roads at Exit 13.
    Gas for cooking is usually bought by the cylinder. When a
cylinder is empty, you should take it for exchange to one of the
many filling points, which are usually unmarked, but easily
identifiable by the rows of gas cylinders standing outside. This
does not cost much: at the time of writing about SR20 for a full
cylinder, which might last a family about a month. The
Sulaimaniya filling point is on the right of Tahlia Street,
Sulaimaniya, between the Can restaurant junction and the
Olaya Road junction, and there are plenty of others.

Water
The water which comes to your house through the taps is a
mixture of well water and desalinated water and can be
safely drunk, although many people prefer to buy bottled
water from the supermarket or to use a filter. The tap water
has sufficient fluoridation to protect children's teeth. A
number of companies, such as Aqua, al-Manhal, and Safia
among others, deliver glass cylinders of drinking water, for
use with an electric water cooler to compounds and villas
on a regular schedule. At the time of writing a new cylinder
costs SR20 while filling it cost only SR6. Sometimes the
electric cooler is offered free as a promotional value.
    Water is currently supplied by the municipality on a half
day on, three days off basis. These days vary from area to
area and change frequently within an area. This should not

Old and new in Riyadh - the water tower seen from the roof of the Murabba Palace

present a problem for household use, as long as householders are sensibly frugal in their use of water, as most villas are supplied with a capacious water tank on the roof. It is sometimes a problem for gardens in the summer, however, and you should be conscious of the need to conserve water and, in particular, you should not over-water the garden. If municipality officers see water flowing under the gate, they can impose a fine on the householder.

Domestic Help

If you plan to employ a maid or other servant, ensure that there is suitable accommodation in the house. Good part-time or full-time domestic staff are readily available. Some families take on a couple, the wife to help in the house and with baby-sitting, the husband to drive. The interests of both employee and employer are best protected if the domestic servant is supplied by a company specialising in this function. Sa'ad al-Rasheed Services Corporation (T) will provide this service.

It is illegal for an employee to work in a house other than that of his sponsor except by agreement with the sponsor.

Sa'ad al-Rasheed
Svcs. Corp.   403 0900

Medical

Hospitals

Government hospitals do not accept non-Saudis, except in an emergency. There are a number of private hospitals, of which the best known are listed below. Most expatriates have their medical expenses covered by an insurance policy taken out by their employer. For treatment at any hospital, payment must be made, or visible means of payment demonstrated, before treatment. For this reason it is a good idea to carry a credit card with you at all times. The following hospitals offer obstetric, paediatric and gynaecological care. Some insurance policies do not cover obstetrics.

▸ *Al Hamadi Hospital* (T), behind al-Akariya shopping centre, Olaya.

The King Faisal Specialist Hospital

▸ *Dallah Hospital* (T), Olaya, King Fahad Highway.
▸ *Al Mishari Hospital* (T), behind al-Jazeerah supermarket, Sulaimaniya.
▸ *Green Crescent Health Services* (T), behind the Intercontinental Hotel.
▸ *The Social Insurance (GOSI) Hospital* (T), near Rabwa market, off Ring Road East, exit 14.

Al-Hamadi Hsp	464 3312
Dallah Hsp	454 5277
Al-Mishari Hsp	464 7700
Green Crescent	464 4434
GOSI	493 3000

Clinics

Most people are attached to a clinic for their general health care, while for specific needs they will consult one of the specialist clinics. Those used by companies and individuals include:

▸ *Ghassan N. Pharaon (GNP) Clinic* (T), Malaaz, on al-Amir Fawwaz ibn Abdul Aziz Street which cuts to the right from al-Ahsa circle when leaving town on Khorais Road, offers a full range of medical and dental services (but not in cases of emergency) and x-ray.
Hours: 9.00 am-1.00 pm and 4.30 pm-8.30 pm
First consultation SR100, subsequent consultations SR50.

▸ *Consulting Clinics* (T), near Azizia supermarket, on Dammam/Makkah Highway, offers the full range of out-patient services and has a staff of specialist consultants, but is not an emergency centre.
Hours: 8.30 am-12.30 pm and 4.00 pm-8.30 pm, Saturday to Wednesday inclusive; 8.30 am-2.00pm and 5.00 pm-8.00 pm Thursday.
First consultation SR125 to 200 plus SR100 for file opening, Follow-up within five days free of charge, Second consultation SR125 to 200.

▸ *Transad Medical and Dental Clinic* (T), in Sulaimaniya, between al-Jazeerah supermarket and Grand Festival Palace, offers, in addition to routine out-patient care and referral to specialist or hospital consultation, the following care: in-house x-ray, obstetrical/gynaecological service, paediatrics, ECG, 24-hour emergency service, physiotherapy and dental service.
Hours: 8.00 am-8.00 pm, Saturday to Wednesday inclusive;

GNP	476 7597
Consulting Clinics	465 9100
Transad Clinic	465 0840

8.00am-12.00 pm and 4.00 pm-8.00pm Thursday.
Dental service: 8.00 am-5.00 pm, Saturday, Sunday and
Tuesday; 8.00 am-7.00 pm Monday and Wednesday.
First consultation SR100, follow-up visits free within five days.

▶ *Specialised Medical Centre* (T), at the intersection of King
Fahad and Khorais Roads, provides all services, including
fully integrated and on-site radiology, laboratory, dental,
opthalmology, and physiotherapy departments. The Centre
also arranges home health care service and same day sugery

▶ *Family Medical Clinic* (T), behind SACO hardware store at end
of al-Aruba Road on King Abdulaziz Street (Old Airport Road).
Hours: 9.00 am-12.30 am and 4.00 pm-9.00 pm.

▶ *Dr. Amal's Paediatric Clinic* (T), behind the Military
Hospital, sees children from birth to the age of 16 (18 in the
case of girls), by appointment. The clinic also offers a health
and beauty service to women.

▶ Chiropractic services are offered at the *Spine and Sports
Injury Clinic* (T) behind the al-Azizia Shopping Center on
Khorais Road,

Specialised Medical Centre	416 4000
Family Medical Centre	465 6263
Dr Amal's Paediatric Clinic	476 0438
Spine & Sports Injury Clinic	480 2360

Dental Services
Before undergoing any dental treatment, it is a good idea to
get an estimate of the cost, especially if you are paying yourself. The clinics above include dentists among their staff; particularly reliable are those in Transad, the Family Medical
Clinic and GNP. In addition there are a few centres specialising in dental treatment.

▶ *GAMA Dental Centre* (T), first floor, FAL shopping centre.
Hours: 7.00am-5.00pm Saturday, Wednesday and Thursday;
7.00am-9.00pm Sunday, Monday and Tuesday.

▶ *Dr. Fatina al-Humoud's dental surgery clinic* (T) in the
Circon Building near al-Akariya shopping centre, Olaya.
Hours: 9.00am-1.00pm and 4.30-8.30pm
First consultation SR100.

▶ *Ramh Dental and Implant Center* (T) also has American
dentists.

GAMA Centre	454 2929
Dr Fatina al-Humoud	465 6425
Ramh Dental & Implant Clinic	488 4084

King Khalid Specialist Eye Hospital

Optical Services

Opticians usually display a pair of spectacles above their door and can supply eyeglasses, contact lenses and other eye products. Most also offer eye testing. Opticians can be found on Olaya Road, Thalateen Sulaimaniya, King Abdulaziz Street (Old Airport Road) and in Ba'tha. Al-Moghreby (T) close to KKESH Eye Hospital and at the intersection of Tahliya and Olaya Roads has a large selection of designer frames. Al-Saleh Eye Care Center (T) off Sitteen Street behind the National Hospital has US certified opthalmologists. Barakat Optical (T) in King Abdulaziz Street and with branches elsewhere, is described as the largest optical center in Riyadh.

Al-Moghreby	488 6156
Al-Saleh Eye Care Centre	478 6660
Barakat Optical	476 9105

Opticians recommend that sunglasses be worn regularly in the strong sunlight of Riyadh. Expensive sunglasses are not medically necessary – any glass will act as a barrier to most ultraviolet light. The cheapest sunglasses will protect the eyes as well as the most expensive. If your eyes begin to water or feel dry on a regular basis, you may have become subject to 'dry eye syndrome'. Opthalmologists often recommend the regular use of a saline eye drop such as Tears Naturale, which is available at any pharmacy.

Mental Health

There are a number of psychologists and psychotherapists available to help both adult expatriates and children. The American Community Services (ACS) (T) has a list of names.

ACS	482 9604

Veterinary Services

These veterinary sevices provide pet vaccinations, neutering, x-rays, PH balanced dog and cat food, and boarding: the Riyadh Veterinary Clinic (T), associated with Jeddah Veterinary Clinic, is off Exit 9 in a new building on the service road; Aman Veterinary Clinic (T) which trains and boards the Security Services dogs, is off Exit 16 on Haroun Rashid Road; the National Veterinary Clinic (T), is at the south end of al-Ahsa (Pepsi) Road; Dr. Maged El Heyek (T), a USA certified veterinarian, makes house calls.

Riyadh Vet. Clinic	456 6376
Aman Vet Clinic	435 8661
National Vet. Clinic	403 3494
Dr Maged El Heyek	486 0459 x 34

Pharmacies

Pharmacies can be found all over the city; they usually display a sign showing a mortar and a snake, often open-mouthed and spitting. Many drugs supplied only on prescription in other countries can be bought over the counter in Riyadh. Larger pharmacies attached to hospitals and clinics often supply a wider range of drugs than the local neighbourhood pharmacy. A list of 24-hour pharmacies with phone numbers is published regularly in *The Riyadh Daily* and can be clipped and kept next to the telephone.

Emergencies

You can dial 997 for an ambulance (998 for fire), but English may not be readily understood. It is much better to call one of the clinics or hospitals above, or just to go to the nearest hospital.

Carry a credit card in case you are asked to demonstrate your ability to pay.

Health Hazards
Snake-bite   This is a much exaggerated danger in Saudi Arabia. Although the Kingdom does have venomous snakes, there is very little danger of being bitten by one of them. Wearing shoes when in the desert will help you avoid any real risk. In the unlikely event of your being bitten, keep the affected limb immobilised and drive as quickly as possible to the nearest hospital. Don't panic! The King Fahad National Guard Hospital is home to the venom extraction center and should be the first hospital to head for in the case of snake bite.

Skin cancer   Westerners coming to Riyadh for the first time are inclined to over-indulge in sunbathing and this is now known to be dangerous. The cumulative effect of too much exposure to the sun may cause skin problems later, as may just one acute case of sunburn. This is especially true of children; early inattention to the need for protection from the sun can result years later in serious skin disease. So expose your body gradually to the sun, if possible restricting your sunbathing to the early morning and evening. Cover yourself and your children with protective creams, sun-blocking lotions if you are fair-skinned. Riyadh is excessively dry and this can also cause problems to the skin, and so you should make generous use of moisturising creams. Remember Riyadh is very close to the Tropic of Cancer.

Opportunities for Women

Many women discover they have the opportunity for leisure in Riyadh. Without a financial obligation to work, women may take up new interests or resume old ones. Through different women's groups sponsored by embassies, women can discover social groups engaged in a variety of sports activities such as tennis and golf, handicraft activities such as quilting and

Al-Nahda Philanthropic Society

embroidery, and intellectual pursuits such as foreign language conversation circles, book discussion groups, and bridge competitions. Classes in various activities such as computer skills and ethnic cooking are offered at ACS and by private teachers. The cultural counsellors at the French Embassy and the German Embassy are good resources for those wishing to pursue the study of those languages. Other resources can be found in the section on adult education on page 62.

However, many women also wish to be gainfully employed. Depending on skills, there are a variety of job opportunities in Riyadh, although government restrictions on women working in the same offices as men remain in place. Qualified teachers, accountants, librarians, and secretaries may be hired by the international schools. Those with qualifications at the masters' level may pursue a teaching job at the women's university while those with English as a Second Language teaching qualifications may teach at one of the numerous language schools or as a private tutor to adults or children eager to learn English.

The hospitals are an exception to the gender-segregation rules and nurses, therapists, doctors, dentists, and others in the health care professions are always in demand, at both hospitals and clinics.

Qualified accountants, lawyers and architects can find employment if they look carefully. One resource is the volunteer-run Professional Women's Network which meets at ACS (T). Many skilled women pursue independent contract or sales work out of their homes, taking advantage of the free-lance nature of the work to establish their own schedules. Others take the opportunity to try something completely different. Expatriate women have successfully engaged in desk-top publishing for newsletters and brochures, travel and trip planning and different types of consignment sales arrangements, particularly on compounds. Women who are fully engaged in handicrafts often find that the compound and organisation bazaars are an outlet for their handmade items, particularly those that are seasonal.

ACS	482 9604

Many expatriate women have seized the opportunity to travel and explore other cultures, both within the Middle East and in Europe and the Far East. While some collect handicrafts and art works only for themselves, others have arranged contacts for import-export businesses based in their home countries.

Women may also volunteer to work with charity organisations or in schools, such as the Down Syndrome Centre run by the al-Nadha Society or the American International School. An enterprising woman who keeps her eyes open and is willing to network can easily occupy her time with a wide variety of activities supported by the local and expatriate community. Volunteers in Riyadh organise performing arts groups, a variety of sports

"Ladies only" design studio

Art Nouveau	416 2990

leagues ranging from softball to roller blade hockey, natural history and exploration groups, and professional working groups for everything from accountants to personal fitness instructors to writers.

Women may also take advantage of the "women only" activities of Riyadh. Lunch with a woman friend at the Art Nouveau Restaurant (T), a visit to one of the women only Internet cafés springing up, or even a walk through one of the many dress shops staffed by women for women will provide insight into local society and its customs.

Opportunities for Men

There are groups of American and British businessmen which meet regularly. For details, contact the Commercial Section of the relevant embassy. There are other national groups and organisations serving the different communities within Riyadh. You should ring the relevant embassy (numbers listed on page 83) and contact the Community Liaison Officer (CLO), if there is one, or the Cultural Attaché or Commercial Section.

Postal Services and Telephones

Stamps are often difficult to obtain in Riyadh. The only certain source is the central Post Office (in which women are not permitted); area offices have stamps only intermittently. Ordinary letters carry a postage of SR1 inland and SR2 overseas. Letters can be registered at the Post Office, at a cost of SR4 or SR5 per letter, depending on weight. Most companies have a franking machine and this can be used for letters. There is no door-to-door mail service in the Kingdom and most individuals receive their mail through company post office boxes at one of the neighbourhood post offices. However, al-Mourouj Postal Services (T) and Mail Boxes Etc. (T) offer private mail boxes for rent as well as shipping supplies and stationery.

Many companies like to entrust their mail to a courier. Several services are now available in Riyadh: DHL/SNAS (T) with headquarters next to French Corner on the road which connects Dabbab Street to the Military Hospital; FedEx (T) on King Fahad Expressway with a branch office in Malaaz; and UPS (T), also on King Fahad Expressway. These services provide pick-up on demand as well as delivery.

Most people receive mail at their company's post office box, as mail is not delivered to houses. Sizable packets or parcels will be opened for inspection, either for censorship or customs, whether sent through the post or by courier. Books may be subject to long delays or confiscation.

The most recent Riyadh telephone directory, with its useful yellow pages, was issued in 1998-9. Telephone and pager service can be initiated by filling out subscription forms at the local office of Saudi Telecom, but new lines are not always available. Keep this in mind when looking for housing as you may want to inquire if a phone line goes with the villa or apartment.

Public telephones can be found outside supermarkets and in prominent positions such as street corners. The best way to pay for calls is by buying phone cards for SR50 or SR100 from the main Post Office. These can be used for both national and international calls. Otherwise the shop, if the phone box is located in or near a shop, will supply coins to the value of SR1 or 50 halalas. Call Cabines are now located all over the city. These offices offer private booths from which long-distance calls can be made and paid for on site.

Al-Mourouj	460 1161
Mail Boxes Etc	461 2047
DHL/SNAS	462 1919
FedEx	419 4220
UPS	800 124 6699

The main Post Office

Internet and E-mail

King Abdul Aziz City for Science and Technology organised the introduction of internet/e-mail services into the Kingdom and continues to monitor their practice. Forty-one companies were approved to offer these services, but only a few actually jumped into the market, Among the most used are Zajil (T), Naseej (T) and Primenet (T). E-mail service is offered for a fixed price: Internet service has a fixed charge per quarter as well as an additional per hour or per minute charge on the Saudi Telecom bill for use of the data only telephone lines.

Zajil	462 1756
Naseej	080 124 1333
Primenet	460 1972

Shopping

Riyadh is well served with shops, and the supermarkets and corner shops *(baqqalas)*, large shopping malls and traditional suqs cover most shopping needs. Mothers with babies and toddlers may like to know that some shopping malls are better adapted than others to manoeuvring a pushchair. The al-Mousa Centre in Olaya Street has fewer steps than some of the other shopping centres and the shops are closer together, so that negotiating the distance between shopping stops is easier.

Opening Times

Shops shut at prayer times *(salah)*. There are five prayer times in each day, each lasting approximately half an hour. All but the dawn prayer *(fajr)* affect the shops: midday *(dhuhr)*, afternoon *(asr)*, sunset *(maghrib)* and evening *(isha)*. These times naturally vary according to the daylight hours; check the exact times on page two of the English-language daily newspapers. Most shops open at about 9.00 am and close for *dhuhr* prayer, reopening at about 4.00 pm, and remaining open for about two hours after *isha* prayer. Supermarkets are

Looking for silver jewellery and other treasures in the Antique suq

open from early in the morning (7.00 or 8.00 am) until midnight or later, closing only for prayer times, seven days a week. In Ramadan, the month of fast, most shops open only for an hour or two in the morning and then from about 9.00 pm (after *isha* prayer) until midnight or later. Supermarkets, however, keep almost normal opening hours in Ramadan.

Women should dress discreetly while out shopping, in long skirts and sleeves to cover their arms and legs. Many western women conform to Saudi style by wearing the *abaya*, a loose black cloak, and covering their hair, particularly in the suqs.

Department Stores
There are a few stores in Riyadh where you can find a range of products under one roof.

‣ *Saudi House* (T), on Thalateen Olaya Street, a branch of British Home Stores, sells many kinds of British products, including clothes, china, toys, luggage, kitchenware, cosmetics and linen, and has a good sale after Ramadan.

‣ *Sawani* (T), with branches in the Nojoud, Mousa, Sahara and Oroba Plaza malls, sells household items and clothes for children and ladies (including such brand names as Escada, Nafnaf, and Laurel).

‣ *Fitaihi* (T), on Sitteen Street, sells all sorts of luxury goods, including jewellery, china, luggage and clothes from Italy, France and Germany, in a glittering setting which is worth a visit for its own sake.

‣ *True Value* (T), on King Fahad Highway, sells a huge variety of goods, all very reasonably priced, including art supplies, electrical goods, gardening tools, other tools, paints (they will mix paints for you), hardware, household wares such as china, glass and kitchen equipment, toys, sports equipment, furniture and stationery.

Saudi House	465 3515
Sawani	441 7106
Fitaihi	478 2012
True Value	476 9099

Dira Square

Old copper and brass objects in the Antique suq.

FADS	456 0697

Tamimi Markets	453 1472
King Fahad Rd	453 1472
FAL	463 3973
Al-Azizia	482 7055
Al-Jazeerah	465 5988
Sarawat	464 6856

▸ *FADS* (T), on Prince Abdullah Street and on al-Fahad Street in Badiya has clothing for all members of the family and a good selection of housewares and accessories.

Supermarkets
These sell a good range of products in addition to food, including china, glass, cutlery, kitchenware, toiletries and electrical goods. Among the best-known are:
▸ *Tamimi Markets (Safeway)* (T), has many locations including FAL shopping centre on King Abdulaziz Street (Old Airport Road), King Fahad Highway, across from al-Faisaliyah Center al-Asha Road close to the intersection with Dammam Highway, the intersection of Thalateen Olaya and Dabbab Streets, Old Airport Road and Rakah, across from King Saud University. Safeway has a good selection of British and other products, such as Irish beef, Dutch veal and American chilled beef.
▸ *Al-Azizia* (T), near the King Faisal Specialist Hospital on the junction of Takhassusi Street and the Dammam/Makkah Highway, has a good selection of food and other goods including some Swedish products.
▸ *Al-Jazeerah* (T), Sulaimaniya, has a particularly good range of kitchen equipment.
▸ *Sarawat* (T), Olaya, has a large store at Oruba Plaza at the junction of Oruba Road and King Fahad Highway with a good selection of fresh fish on Sundays, Tuesdays, and Thursdays and a range of European cheeses.
▸ *Panda* (T), has many locations throughout the city, including Thalateen Olaya Street, Aruba Road, and Dammam Highway

in Naseem and Malaaz.

▶ *Euromarché*, on the corner of Takhassusi and Aruba Road, is convenient for the Diplomatic Quarter and has a particularly wide range of products.

▶ *Food Basket* (T), on the Dammam Road by the Rawda 3 exit, is convenient for those living in compounds to the east of Riyadh. A second location has opened on King Fahad Expressway for those living in the center of Riyadh.

▶ *The Oriental Supermarket*, one block behind and to the left of Alphagraphics, stocks ingredients for Oriental cooking, particularly Korean, Japanese and Thai.

Panda	
Aruba Rd.	465 3221
Thalateen Olaya Street	464 4992
Food Basket	231 0113
Oriental Supermarket	463 4076

Shopping Centres or Malls

Well-appointed buildings dedicated to shoppers are located all over Riyadh. They offer a wide range of shops selling clothes, stationery, shoes, jewellery, gifts, pharmaceutical supplies, electrical goods and so on. Since stores go in and out of business, take a small notebook with you when you go to a mall and mark down the shops that warrant a second visit. Soon you will have a list of favourites for everything from sneakers to porcelain. These are the most well-known shopping centres:

Al-Akariya, Olaya, on Olaya Road.
Al-Akariya, Sitteen Street.
Shola, King Abdulaziz Street (Old Airport Road).
Al-Andalus, Olaya Road, near Aruba Road.
FAL, King Abdulaziz Street (Old Airport Road).
Al-Mousa, Olaya Road.
Al-Nojoud, near the Intercontinental Hotel. (Passing the hotel on your right and turning right at the next lights, it is immediately on your left behind SAMA.)
Al-Oruba Plaza, Aruba Road, at junction with King Fahad Highway.
Mejdi Mall, at exit 15 on the Ring Road
The National Products Center, on the King Fahad Expressway, is a purpose-built showcase for Saudi-made consumer products. Store items range from leather jackets and shoes to household cleaners, from sweets and fruit juices to gold jewellery and foam cushions, from house hold appliances to heavy machinery. A walk through the center is educational as well as productive. Many prices are wholesale rather than retail.
Riyadh Sahara Mall, anchored by a Tamimi Safeway super marked and al-Sawani Department Store, at Prince Abdullah and Airport Roads.

Wholesale Shopping

Wholesale outlets for groceries, linens, and clothes are appearing in many parts of the city. Al-Othaim has several locations including the Ring Road between exits 14 and 15 and the new Dira suq. MAX store (T) specialising in whole-

MAX	235 3650

sale groceries, linens, and appliances, operates off Dammam Highway past Naseem. The wholesale outlet of Panda/al-Azizah is in Malaaz, not far from Ba'tha.

Al Sadhan garment center is located off the Ring Road between exits 13 and 14. This store stocks a range of clothes from designer labels to cheap Chinese imports. Check each garment carefully for quality.

Wholesale toys can be found by turning on to Imam Torkey ibn Abdullah ibn Mohammed Street from Ba'tha Street, passing Musmak Palace on your left, and taking the second right hand turn. The shops in the area sell packets of toys and party hats and favours; it is an excellent place to shop for birthday and holiday celebrations. On the next block of Imam Torkey ibn Abdullah ibn Mohammed Street and continuing along the right-hand turn at the next light are many wholesale stationery shops and some wholesale tailor supply stores.

The Gold suq

Suqs

Certainly the most enjoyable way to shop in Riyadh is to spend time in the different suqs, each part of which specialises in a certain product or type of product. It takes time to get to know your way round but it is time well spent. It is best to go to the suqs in the morning.

▸ *Dira Antique suq*, next to Dira Square, is an atmospheric suq selling a variety of old copper and brass objects and carpets. The few truly Arabian products and artefacts include silver daggers *(khanjars)*, silver Bedouin jewellery and dresses, wooden camel-milk bowls, decorated wooden windows and doors, boldly striped orange and brown rugs and old coins. Many of the objects on sale are from India, and some are brand new (such as the brass lanterns which make such a good buy for the garden). The main passage into the suq always smells of sandalwood, many types of which can be found here, together with frankincense and myrrh. Along the same alley and along passages to the left, you will find a good selection of antique carpets, kilims and camel bags. Be sure to bargain! Occasionally you will come across an open air auction of, for example, old daggers *(khanjars)*.

In the same suq you can find the regular Arab male garments – the shirt reaching to the feet *(thobe)*, headdress *(kufiyyah* and *gutra)*, gold-edged wool cloak *(bisht)* and, in summer time, leather sandals. In the cooler months you will see a good selection of fur-lined wool cloaks *(furwa)*, excellent for the desert on a cold evening when sitting round a camp fire.

▸ *Women's suq* is under the multi-storey car-park behind Dira. Here you will find Bedouin women selling bunches of baroque pearls (a good buy), Bedouin jewellery, baskets and spices.

▸ *Ba'tha suq*, to either side of Ba'tha road, offers a wide range

The *furwa*

Baskets for sale in the Women's suq

of electrical goods, clothes (including Kashmiri shawls), spices and kitchen equipment. In the winter, woollen underwear, scarves, gloves, and hats appear. There is a section specialising in hubble-bubble pipes.

▸ *Tent suq* is on a small road running parallel to the main Ba'tha road (behind and a little south of the Ba'tha Hotel). Here you can buy large, white, canvas Pakistani tents with bamboo poles, or have the same material made into useful bags for carrying sleeping-bags, etc., for camping in the desert, or bags for carrying tools of various sorts, sand-ladders or tentpegs. Ready-made shoulder bags, rucksacks, long sausage-shaped bags useful for travelling, and bags of other shapes and sizes can be bought here for next to nothing. Bags can be run up while you wait; you specify the size and shape. In fact canvas or thick cotton covers can be made to cover almost anything!

‣ *Gold suq*, on Tumeiri Street, on the left, looking towards Dira Square and the Clock Tower, is an Aladdin's cave of glittering objects made of gold, some quite ornate and others simpler. The cost of gold items is measured by the weight of gold used, nothing extra is added for workmanship. Some shops sell expensive watches (such as Rolex) second-hand. Indian and Pakistani handicrafts, including papiermaché and carved wood and stone objects, can be found by walking up Tumeiri Street, keeping the gold suq on your left, and checking the different alleyways. The pure cotton fluffy white haj towels and a rainbow of gold-threaded Kashmiri shawls can also be found in this area.

‣ *Kuwaiti suq, suq Owais* and *Taiba suq* between them cover an extensive area between the Olaya Road and King Fahad Highway, going north out of the city. They are useful sources of all sorts of kitchenware, cutlery and crockery, camping stuff, toys and children's clothing, and electrical goods, all very cheaply priced. You can also find dress material and bedding, including quilts and blankets (none of which, however, will be wool) and some clothing, particularly *abayas*.

‣ *Suq as Semak*, or fish suq, in the area behind the Murabba Palace, sells fresh fish from the Arabian Gulf, which arrives on Saturday, Monday, Wednesday and Thursday.

‣ *Haraj*, or second-hand suq, in the large area to the right of Ba'tha Street just before it meets the Ring Road at junction 21, offers all sorts of second-hand clothing, furniture and many other things. You could furnish a complete house adequately, if not fashionably, and very cheaply here. It is a useful source of such things as children's bicycles, floor cushions and other furniture for a 'majlis'. There are things you never realised you needed and plenty of glittery dresses for children's dressing-up games. Some of the rugs are antique. The suq takes place in the open air every afternoon from 4.00 pm (except on Thursdays and Fridays when it opens at 2.00 pm) until dark or after *isha* prayer.

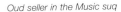
Oud seller in the Music suq

‣ *Vegetable and fruit suqs* sell produce at wholesale prices and in large quantities, which is useful for large families or groups of families sharing. There is one at Rabwa by exit 14 of the Ring Road. Suq al-Shamal (north suq) at Mursalat also sells fruit and vegetables. There are a few open-air fruit and vegetable stalls in Thalateen Sulaimaniya Street.

‣ *Suq al-Hammam,* or pigeon market, is a fascinating place to observe an old Saudi tradition, the display and purchase of all kinds of birds, including hawks, which can be seen sitting hooded on their perches. There is even the occasional peacock. This market takes place every afternoon after 4.00 pm, in the open air behind the multi-storey car-park behind Dira suq.

‣ *Musical instruments suq,* a charming little area, is to be found off Ba'tha Street, turning left under the second flyover and then immediately forking right. On your right is a large open-air car-park and mosque, on your left a few shops selling hubble-bubble water-pipes (shisha), and unglazed pottery vases and pots. Up a little narrow alley behind the shisha shops are a number of shops selling new traditional musical instruments – drums, pipes (mismah), single-string guitars (rababah) and the lovely Arabian lute (oud).

Auctions

Arts & Antiques Auctioneers Ltd (T), owned by Faisal al-Saddawy Trading Establishment, holds four auctions a year in Riyadh at the Cultural Center of the Diplomatic Quarter with companion auctions in Jeddah, Dubai, Kuwait, and Qatar. Arts and Antiques specialises in Middle Eastern artifacts, arms, glass, and manuscripts and also trades in Orientalist paintings and European art works. Faisal al-Saddawy will continue to operate a small art and antique shop at his former location off Olaya Road opposite the UNDP offices.

Arts & Antiques 464 8182

Shopping by Product

Art supplies   Al-Marsam (T), on the first floor of the al-Akariya shopping centre (on the left at the top of the first staircase) sells a good range of materials for the artist. For the serious artist in search of specific supplies, House of Talents (T) opposite al-Akariya Mall, and Jarir Bookshop (T) are excellent sources. Excellent and reasonably priced framers with a wide range of framing styles abound in Riyadh. The Village (T), on Thalateen Olaya Street, Sharqia Art Supplies (T), in the Diplomatic Quarter, Zamani (T), opposite Panda on Sulaimaniya Thalateen and also on Olaya, can all be recommended for framing. ADEL stores (T), with four branches in Riyadh, sells a wide variety of craft kits as well as all the supplies for cross-stitch, needlepoint, and other decorative arts.

Al-Marsam	464 4374
House of Talents	465 9073
Jarir	462 6000
The Village	463 4211
Sharqia	488 0872
Zamani	461 6225
ADEL	464 5878

Antiques   Raking through the piles of old copper, brass and wooden objects in the Dira Antique suq is one of the most enjoyable ways of looking for either real antiques or just attractive old objects, and you may chance upon some real treasures. Faisal al-Saddawy's Arts and Antiques (T), mentioned under Auctions, sells beautiful objects with prices to match.

Faisal al-Sadday's
Arts & Antiques 464 8182

Bicycles   You can buy new bicycles from Wheels (T) in Thalateen Sulaimaniya Street or at Ba'tha Suq in the small bicycle shops behind the multi-story carpark or in Five Building, and second-hand bikes from the second-hand suq (see page 34). True Value (T) on King Fahad Highway also sells bicycles. Bicycles can be repaired by Wheels, who will also sell you parts and accessories, and by Red Sea Divers (T). In your neighbourhood you may find a hole-in-the-wall bicycle repair shop to repair punctures; these are often advertised by the bicycle wheels hanging outside.

Wheels	464 3321
True Value	476 9099
Red Sea Divers	450 0365

Jarir	462 6000
Al-Shegrey	462 8684
Obeikan	465 0129
Al-Maktaba	
Malaz	476 1597
Olaya	464 4065
Al-Marikh	464 7531
	465 8523
Dar al-Uloum	477 7121
	477 1952

Picnic	450 0088
True Value	476 9099
SACO	464 6700

Carpet World	
Old Airport Rd	478 6829
Olaya Rd	464 5419
Oriental Carpet	
Bazaar	477 7782
Les Chateaux	476 5559
Nawras Nest	
Old Airport Rd	478 1881
Olaya Rd	465 6222

Books and Stationery   Jarir Bookshop (T) has three branches: Olaya Road close to al-Akariya Mall, and on al-Ahsa Road next to Safeway, and Prince Abdullah Road. Jarir has a wide selection of books, with a particularly good section on Arabia and the Middle East. It also stocks office furniture, computers and computer supplies, office stationery, children's toys and educational books. With an SR500 purchase shoppers can obtain a card offering a 10% discount on all future purchases. Al-Shegrey Bookstore (T), behind Jarir Bookshop, has much the same stock. Tihamah has lots of branches: in al-Akariya centre, Olaya, opposite FAL shopping centre on King Abdulaziz Street (Old Airport Road), on Olaya Road near the al-Mousa centre, and on Dabbab Street nearly opposite the Saudi-British Bank. It has a wide selection of English-language books. Obeikan (T), at the junction of King Fahad Highway and Aruba Road, has behind its vast selection of Arabic books a good choice of English-language textbooks and classics, and a few maps and Blue Guides. Al-Maktaba (T), of which there are several branches, has a good range of stationery and office equipment. Al-Marikh (T), off the Olaya Road just past the crossing of the Dammam/Makkah Highway, has a good selection of educational books, including English-language teaching books. Dar al-Uloum (T) in al-Akariya shopping centre, Sitteen Street, is good for educational books.

In general, English classics are hard to come by in Riyadh but many used book stores have opened in the city and offer some intriguing choices in their English sections.

Camping and Picnic Equipment   Picnic (T) on Olaya Road past the Kuwaiti suq offers one-stop shopping for camping, desert driving, and picnicking in the dunes. Even sand ladders can be found here.The supermarkets, especially Euromarché, sell tables, chairs, cool-boxes and a lot of other things useful for camping and picnics. The Tent suq, in addition to tents and tent poles, has a variety of useful bags, and canvas covers with lots of zips to cover equipment boxes. The major hardware stores such as True Value (T) on King Fahad Highway and SACO (T) in its various locations are a good source for pop-up tents, camp stoves, propane lamps and picnic ware. Camping and picnic materials designed specifically for desert camping, such as windscreens for fire, can also be found off the Ring Road around exits 14 and 15.

Carpets   It is fun to seek out oriental carpets in the carpet suq at Dira, if you know what you are looking for and are prepared to bargain. Carpet shops such as Carpet World (T), Oriental Carpet Bazaar (T), Les Châteaux (T) and Nawras Nest (T) can be found on Abdulaziz Street and Olaya Roads. The shop owners will often let you "borrow" a rug for a week of two to test how it fits in with your lifestyle and décor. The carpet shop in the Intercontinental Hotel has a good choice of rugs at reasonable prices. Silk Roads (T) in the old al-Akariya shopping mall on Sitteen Street has an excellent selection of silk carpets.

Silk Roads	472 1620

Rugs, kilims and camel bags in the Carpet suq

China and Glass   Villeroy and Bosch and Heinrich china and porcelain can be found at SARA (T) at the crossroads of Olaya Road and Tahlia Street and on Sitteen Street. Wedgwood is sold by Saudi House (T) on Thalateen Olaya Street. Royal Doulton china is sold at the Hakbani Centre (T) on the corner of Takhassusi and Prince Sultan Bin Abdulaziz Streets. Check out the coffee mugs with the Arabian nights scene. Kuwaiti suq (*see* page 34) and al-Mejdi mall at Exit 15 on the Ring Road have good cheap china and glass shops. Rosenthal china is to be found in Le Cygne Commercial Centre, Thalateen Olaya Street (opposite Forsans). Fitaihi (T), on Sitteen Street, has many varieties of china and glass. Everything you need for your dinner-party table can be bought in a lovely French shop in Thalateen Olaya Street, Geneviève Lethu (T).

SARA	463 2693
Saudi House	465 3515
Hakbani Centre	481 2068
Fitaihi	478 2012
Geneviève Lethu	464 1959

Clothes: Children   Shops come and go so quickly, but Olaya Road, al-Mousa Mall and al-Akariya Sitteen have a good selection of children's clothes stores. Kickers/Floriane (T) on Olaya Road opposite al-Akariya Shopping Centre has beautiful French clothes and shoes. Mothercare (T) has 100 per cent cotton clothes in the al-Nemer Centre next door. Kid's Kingdom has outlets at al-Akariya Olaya and next to FADS on Prince Abdullah Street. Splash (T), across from Jarir Bookstore, and Guess (T), on Olaya as well as at shopping centres, cater to the teenage girl and boy. Benetton (T) is close to the corner of Olaya and Khorais Road. Ladybird (T), which sells British clothes, Adams (T) and

Kickers/Floriane	464 8911
Mothercare	465 1803
Kid's Kingdom	463 4141
Splash	419 6836
Guess	465 3754
Benetton	462 6871
Ladybird	461 1826
Adams	461 1853

Chicco	462 4043
Jacadi	478 4414
Sawani	441 7106

Chicco (T) which specialises in Italian children's wear, are located in the al-Mousa Mall. The al-Akariya Mall on Sitteen Street also has outlets for Ladybird, Adams, and Jacadi (T) with a French line of children's clothing. S'MAA on Khorais Road outside the Ring Road and Sawani (T) in the Nojoud, Mousa, Sahara, and Oruba shopping centres have casual clothing for the whole family as well as a wide selection of children's clothes. Children's clothes can also be found in supermarkets such as Euromarché, and suqs, especially the Kuwaiti suq.

Tumeiri Street and the Clock Tower

Clothes: Adult   The choice of clothes shops in Riyadh is good, with new shops and boutiques constantly opening. The building of the al-Faisaliyah Centre initiated widespread renovation and reconstruction in the Olaya area; many shops have moved into expanded quarters and al-Ajlan is opening a string of new boutiques on King Fahad Highway. Note that trying on clothes in shops visited by both men and women is not permitted. These shops will normally allow customers to take clothes home on approval and then either exchange the item or have their money back. There are, however, fitting rooms for ladies in ladies-only shops and for men in men-only shops.

It is difficult to keep abreast of shops selling clothes. New smart shops with well-known designer names are opening every week, on the streets where such boutiques are most concentrated – Thalateen Olaya Street, Tahlia Street, Olaya Road and King Fahad Highway. It is best to keep an eye on these streets to catch the new arrivals. The Circon Building alongside al-Akariya shopping centre, Olaya, contains a number of good shops for both men and women, and in the street behind there are three or four ladies-only shops selling good designer clothes.

While it is invidious to select, it may be useful to mention a few shops selling designer clothes, in most of which you may try clothes on. In the Circon Building are Okarina (T) and Mayas for women, Bleu Marine (T) and Gianni Versace (T) for men; on Thalateen Olaya Street there is Christian Dior (T) for both men and women. Giorgio Armani and Salvatore Ferragamo (T), Kenzo (T), Gianfranco Ferre (T) and Prima Donna (T) which has clothes from the Ungaro, Fendi, and Moschino labels, are on Olaya Road.. In June many of these shops have sales. The Outfit Mall on Nosayr Road has a wide selection of British clothes for women while Mee Mees Cottons (T) on Olaya close to Tahlia Street specialises in pure cotton clothes from India and elsewhere. Diane Frès dresses are sold by Lilac (T) in Olaya (turn right at the north end of Thalateen Sulaimaniya Street and you will see it on your right). Al-Multaka (T), in Malaaz, not far from the Commission for Yanbu and Jubail in al-Ahsa (Pepsi) Road, has a selection of top-of-the-range haute-couture clothes for women only, in a very attractive setting. Al-Ajlan (T) at al-Mousa Mall has a wide selection of European mens' suits, dress shirts, and ties and a second outlet at al-Akariya Olaya (T).

Some familiar brand names and branches of western chain stores can be found in Riyadh. French Connection (T) and Liz Claiborne (T) are in the al-Nemer Centre on Olaya Road facing al-Akariya Mall. Sisley and other English shops can be found at the Outfit Mall on Nosayr Street, around the corner from al-Nemer. Mexx (T) and Benetton(T) are on Olaya Road. You will find Wrangler and Lee jeans in Western Cowboy (T) in Oruba Plaza, al-Akariya and al-Shola Malls, and copies of other well-known makes of jeans in Ba'tha suq. Saudi House (T) on Thalateen Olaya is a branch of BHS and has many items familiar to British shoppers. While you cannot try clothes on in most of these shops, some compounds have excellent boutiques of womens' clothes, such as Arabesque (T) in the Arab Investment Compound, and there you may try the clothes.

Okarina	465 6622
Bleu Marine	465 9560
Versace	462 7493
Christian Dior	464 5696
Gianfranco Ferre	465 8527
Ferragamo	465 4322
Kenzo	464 9317
Western Cowboy	419 1259
Lamsa	460 1214
Saudi House	465 3515
Prima Dona	462 4995
Lilac	462 9420
Al-Multaka	478 3388
Al-Ajlan	465 8430
Al-Akariya	465 8430
Liz Claiborne	462 4322
Mexx	461 5934
Benetton	462 6871
Arabesque	482 3444 x 270

Computers   With Internet and e-mail services available in Kingdom, a home computer may be the easiest way to stay in touch with family and friends in other countries. Al-Jeraisy (T) on King Fahd Expressway sells and services IBM, Compaq, and Apple computers. Jarir Bookstores (T) has a wide selection of personal computers and software as well as computer accessories. The computer suq is located around the intersection of Khorais Road and Olaya Road toward the al-Andalusia

Al-Jeraisy	462 3030
Sales ext:	1181
Service ext:	2817
Jarir Bookstores	462 6000

Restaurant. Here you can bargain to your heart's content, buy some nifty computer gadgets, and look for hard-to-find computer accessories.

Electronic Goods   Shathly Electronics (T) in al-Akariya Centre, Olaya, and the many stores at al-Shola Mall, which can make cords to fit specific appliances, are a reliable source of electronic goods. Ba'tha has a cheaper selection in the 'Five Buildings', beneath the Ba'tha Hotel on the left as you go south down Ba'tha street.

Shathly Elec.	464 6911

Fabrics   Dressmaking materials are abundant and reasonably priced in Riyadh. Mutanabbe Street in Malaaz is a covered pedestrian street, prettily laid out and devoted solely to shops selling fabrics. It runs parallel to Sitteen Street to the left as you go south beyond al-Akariya shopping centre, Sitteen. The Fabrics suq, to the right of Tumeiri Street as you look down it towards the Clock Tower, is another area given over to dress-making fabric shops. *See also* Services: Tailors and Dressmakers, page 49.

Rather more expensive fabrics can be found in the numerous material shops in the shopping centres, especially al-Akariya, Olaya.

Florists   One of the delights of living in Riyadh is the abundance of good florists. By each hospital there is a good flower shop. Planters (T) has its main store with a large selection of cut flowers and indoor plants beween the DHL offices and the French Corner restaurant close to the Military Hospital and has branch shops in every Tamimi Safeway Supermarket. Ashtal, the garden centre, on Abdullah bin Abdulaziz Street near its junction with King Abdulaziz Street, also sells indoor plants. Desert Rose (T), in the Nojoud centre, has an excellent choice of cut flowers and indoor plants. Rosa (T), has branches next to SACO Hardware on King Abdulaziz Street, by Hammadi Hospital and in the Military Hospital. Rosa acts as agent for Interflora and credit card orders for flowers to be delivered worldwide can be placed by telephoning 463 4023. Beautiful Gardens (T) at Takasussi and Mousa Bin Nusair Streets. and the Sultan Garden Centre (T) on Takhassusi Street stock vases as well as flowers and also deal in small pets and birds.

Planters	465 9986
Desert Rose	441 8748
Rosa	464 1203
Beautiful Gdns	464 0102
Sultan Gdn Cent.	465 5555 ext 275

Food   In addition to the supermarkets mentioned above, there are plenty of corner shops in the residential areas which sell basic foodstuffs. There are also some speciality shops.
▸ *Meat:* Forsan (T), on Thalateen Olaya Street near its junction with Dabbab Street.
▸ *Fish:* Fish can be bought fresh from Saudi Fisheries (T), which has branches throughout the city and in major supermarkets. Fresh fish, including fresh salmon, comes to Sarawat supermarket (T) twice a week.

Forsan	465 9144
Saudi Fisheries	462 4741
Sarawat Supermarket	463 3809

▸ *Chocolates and cake:* French Corner (T), on Dabbab Street, on the corner of the road leading to the Military Hospital, has a good French bakery and patisserie. It is also a restaurant (*see* page 56). Thalateen Olaya Street is a centre for chocolates and pastries. Le Gourmet (T),with a branch on Sitteen Street, Le Nôtre (T), Patchi (T) with exquisite trays of beautifully wrapped chocloates, and Neuhaus Chocolates (T) offer beautiful set pieces for a dinner party dessert or for a hostess or housewarming gift. Cheesecake Factory (T), offers a variety of cheesecakes, complete or by the piece, at its outlet in the al-Azizia shopping area on Khorais Road.

▸ *Lebanese or Arab pastries:* There are many places to buy these, including the supermarkets, especially during Ramadan when other shops are shut. Among the best shops is Honey Comb Sweets, on the junction of Olaya Road and Thalateen Olaya Street, and Saadeddin which has branches in Thalateen Olaya Street, King Abdulaziz Street (Old Airport Road), and Khorais Road.

▸ *Dates:* Al-Bateel (T), which has branches in Thalateen Olaya Street (almost opposite Saudi House) and in al-Akariya centre, Olaya, and Kingdom Dates (T) on Olaya Road specialise in the many varieties of Saudi dates, an excellent gift when visiting Saudi homes. These stores also sell date confections garnished with chocolates or nuts and chilled fresh dates, a remarkable taste treat.

Health food and health products: GNC (General Nutrition Centre) (T), with branches in Thalateen Olaya Street and al-Ahsa (Pepsi) Street, in the Tamimi Safeway complex and in the two al-Azizia shopping centres, sells a complete range of multi-vitamins, minerals and herbs as well as energy-producing products for athletes, products for those on diets and herbal treatments for some chronic ailments. It offers a 'Gold Card' for SR75, which entitles the bearer to a 20 percent dis-

French Corner	464 5322
Le Gourmet	
Olaya St	465 4737
Sitteen St	476 3114
Le Nôtre	465 1465
Patchi	465 9768
Neuhaus Choc.	462 1555
Cheescake Fact.	488 3309
Al-Bateel	462 6019
Kingdom Dates	462 2444
GNC	463 3257

Baking Arabic bread (khoubz)

41

Tutti Naturale	465 1755
Oasis	464 2512
The Picnic Stop	450 0088

count on all full-price products on the first Tuesday of each month. Tutti Naturale (T) on Olaya Road, near where it crosses over the Dammam/Makkah Highway, sells health foods and natural products and has a line of foods for diabetics. Oasis (T) in Thalateen Olaya Street, near the junction with Dabbab Street, sells health products, some vitamins and herbs.

▸ *Delicatessen:* Halwani, on Dabbab Street, Sitteen Street and Olaya sells Lebanese food, including a wide range of salads and appetizers. The Picnic Stop (T) in the al-Khozama offers gourmet food to go for picnics as well as convenience foods from the al-Khozama restaurants, such as pesto sauce from Da Pino's.

▸ *Fruit and vegetables:* These can, of course, be bought from the supermarkets, but to obtain fresher and cheaper produce, try buying in bulk from one of the big wholesale vegetable suqs, such as Rawda or the central market Uteiga where most vendors speak Arabic only, or from the little fruit and vegetable stalls in Thalateen Sulaimaniya Street.

▸ *Ice-cream:* Baskin Robbins can be found all over the city. Haagen-Dazs ice creams are available at the Burger King on al-Ahsa (Pepsi Road). TCBY frozen yoghurts are also on al-Ahsa. Both Baskin Robbins and TCBY sell ice cream cakes for special celebrations.

Al-Watania	496 1749

▸ *Organic:* Al-Watania Organic Produce, located between the Rabwah vegetable and ruit markets at Exit 14 and the plastic suqs, has seasonal pesticide-free organic produce grown with natural fertilisers.

Furniture   IKEA (T), on Abdullah ibn Abdulaziz Street, on the left before you see the entrance to King Saud University on your right, has a very good selection of Scandinavian furniture and everything for the home. In fact you could very well set up your home here. The IKEA warehouse also has excellent monthly sales. ID Design (T) on Aruba Street, before it reaches Euromarché, also has bright, modern

IKEA	488 3233
ID Design	462 6159
Al-Mutlaq	465 1835
Wardeh	463 0731
Beity	465 5449
Habitat	465 9877

designs. Al-Mutlaq Furniture (T) offers more traditional furniture designs. There are many branches, including one on Olaya Road near the junction with Tahlia Street. American Homes, on King Fahad Highway just north of its junction with Aruba Street, offers American furniture. There are other large furniture shops nearby. Another good area is Tahlia Street, where you will find Wardeh (T) and Beity (T) among others. Beity will cover furniture (*see also* under Services: Upholstery and Furnishings, page 50). Habitat (T), on Olaya Road,

Monument at the Dabbab Street/Thalateen Olaya Street Intersection

also has furniture to suit the western taste. Dunia al-Beit (T) on Sitteen Street has a beautiful collection of Italian Glass and home accessories as well as furniture. Home Plaza (T) at the intersection of Khorais Road and King Fahad and Home Centre on Tahlia Street (T) stock everything for home and garden from beds and lamps to candles picnic tables, and ceramic planters. For special handmade items with a Mediterranean flavour, try Pottery Plus (T) on Dabbab Street. The constantly changing collection includes rustic furniture, hand-painted pottery, handwoven fabrics, and unusual serving dishes.

Dunia al-Beit	479 1322
Home Plaza	462 5781
Pottery Plus	461 3213

Gardening Supplies   Plants for the garden can be bought from the open-air stalls in Rawda, just off the Dammam/Makkah Highway. Leave the Highway at the exit marked Rawda 3. Earthenware pots can be found in shops along King Fahad Highway, just south of the Ring Road, going south in the direction of Dirab, and in the Musical instruments suq (*see* page 34). Al-Moghtara Farms (T) out toward Dir'iyyah will not only sell you garden plants, but also give you good advice on care in the desert climate. Sultan Garden Centre (T) on Takasussi Street and Home Plaza (T) also offer a wide variety of planters. SACO (T) stocks seeds for both flowers and vegetables.

Al-Moghtara Farms	462 8363
Sultan Gdn Cent.	465 5555
Home Plaza	465 3939
SACO	464 6700

Gifts   If you are looking for something special to give as a gift, there are two shops under the same management, in al-Akariya shopping centre, Olaya, where traditional and modern Arabian and European artefacts in silver, wood and embroidered cloth are sold. The bigger of the two, Lamsa (T), is on the first floor of the old building; the smaller, Badawia (T), is by the bridge which connects the old and new buildings of al-Akariya. The Dira Antique and Kuwaiti suqs (*see* pages 32 and 34) are also good sources of gifts.

Lamsa	460 1214
Badawia	464 3637
Al-Nahda Cent.	478 2583
Bazar Assafarat	48 0627

   The main al-Nahda Centre (T) has a gift shop displaying the Special Rehabilitation Centre products as well as donated gifts and products. The textile centre will make beautiful reproductions of Saudi dresses or modern styles and incorporating Saudi embroidery and beading to order. There is a gift shop in the Diplomatic Quarter called Bazar Assafarat (T). The Chinatown gift shops in al-Mousa (T), al-Akariya (T), and Euromarché (T) shopping centres sell lovely cotton tablecloths, silk shirts, pyjamas, and embroidered pillows. Other branches are at Food Basket and Tumeiry Street

Chinatown	
Al-Mousa	465 8021
Al-Akariya	419 1263

Central Piazza in the Diplomatic Quarter

Fraihi	478 0965
	x 22
Dr al-Angal	462 8197

Funoon Accessories	
	419 0916
ADEL	
Malaaz	476 1543
Al-Shola	478 2471
Olaya Cercon	464 5878
Olaya Main Rd	462 5882

Fitaihi	478 2012
Memory Lane	462 5666
	x 1207
Ruby Jewellers	476 6443

Port Store	463 3169

opposite the gold suq. Fraihi (T), a travel agency in Arba'een Street, off Sitteen Street, Malaaz, can arrange to show you a catalogue of beautiful Syrian inlaid wooden boxes and tables. Dar al-Angal (T) on King Fahad Expressway has Kashmiri handicrafts such as handwoven carpets, papiermaché ornaments, brass objets d'arts and embroideries.

Haberdashery   Sewing needs, such as buttons, thread and a wide variety of other materials, can be supplied by two excellent shops in al-Akariya shopping centre, Olaya. One, the Golden Thread, is situated on the second floor in the old building, by the escalator. The other, called Funoon Acessories (T), is on the first floor of the new building and can be found by going up the first escalator, turning sharp left and then bearing right. The shop is the third on the right. The four ADEL stores in Malaaz (T), al-Shola (T), Olaya Cercon Building (T) and Olaya Main Road (T) next to Alphagraphics, have trimmings, buttons and quilting and craft supplies. Ba'tha suq in the alleys around the mosque and opposite the gold shops has an amazing supply of beads and buttons.

Jewellery and Watches   Torq in the major shopping malls (costume jewellery), the gold shops in some shopping malls, notably al-Akariya centre, Olaya, and of course the Gold suq, sell gold and other items of jewellery. At the women's suq, behind Dira Square, you can bargain with the Bedouin ladies who have strings of baroque pearls from Bahrain and India. The al-Othaim store in al-Akariya Mall Olaya has beautiful strings of matched cultured pearls as well as oversize pearls from the South Seas. A good selection of watch shops can be found in Tumeiri Street, near Dira Square, but you will also find shops in all the shopping malls selling well-known brands at reasonable prices. Fitaihi (T), on Sitteen Street, sells jewellery aimed at the top end of the market. Jewellers at shop # 18 and 20 in the Gold Suq on Tumeiri Street and Memory Lane (T) in the Sahara Towers will cut and set desert diamonds, a type of quartz found locally in the desert, as will the jewellers in the Intercontinental Hotel. Ruby Jewellers (T) on Salah al Din al Ayoubi Road has a large selection of stones from Sri Lanka and elsewhere and has a jewellery designer on staff to help you design a special piece; they will also repair broken pieces. Many of the shops in the Gold suq will copy designs you bring them. The jewellers in the Intercontinental Hotel , will also do this.

Kitchen Equipment and Hardware   Supermarkets have a good selection of kitchenware, china, glass, etc., as does the Kuwaiti suq (*see* page 34). Port Store (T) in Olaya Road has a selection of kitchenware, cutlery and china. SACO Hardware, with probably the largest selection of hardware in Riyadh, has its main branch on King Abdulaziz Street (Old Airport Road), not far from the FAL shopping centre (T), and two other branches, one by the Food Basket on the Dammam Highway in Rawda (T), and the other on Takhassusi Road, just around the corner from Azizia supermarket (T). Here you will find a wide range of kitchen equipment, hardware, some camping and gardening equipment and some car tools and equipment. True Value (T) on King Fahad Highway has a good, cheap range of hardware and DIY material, and the American Sears company has an outlet for its household and garden appliances in Zaina (T) on al-Ahsa (Pepsi) Road. Al-Wani, marked with an enormous *dallah* or Arabic coffee pot, on Khorais Road also has a large selection of kitchen supplies.

SACO	
Main branch	464 6700
Rawda	233 2463
Al-Aziza	248 5899
True Value	476 9099
Zaina/Sears	477 2155

Music   CDs and cassettes are sold by 747 (T), on the junction of Olaya Road and Tahlia Street, and a very good selection of classical and other CDs can be found at Musicmaster (T), just off the King Fahad Highway, opposite al-Faisaliyah Tower. At neither of these shops, however, are women allowed. However, music tapes can usually be bought at the small shops surrounding the supermarkets. Dawaliyah (T), with branches at Oruba and al-Akariya Sitteen Malls, distributes acoustic and electric guitars, drums sets, keyboards and synthesizers, and usually has guitar strings and cases. Shola shopping centre on King Abdulaziz Steet (Old Airport Road) offers a wide variety of musical instrument shops. Yamaha pianos, synthesisers, brass instruments, guitars and drums are sold by Ash-Sharq Distribution (T), located on the ground floor at the back right. On the same floor, but to the left, you will find other shops with some musical instruments. For traditional Arabian instruments, *see* page 34.

747	463 2291
Musicmaster	465 5190
Dawaliya	479 4507
Ash-Sharq Dist.	479 1791

Perfume and Cosmetics   On Thalateen Olaya Street are two large shops, Bugshan (T) and Gazzaz (T), selling many brands of perfume and cosmetics. Saudi House (T) and Fitaihi (T) are also good sources for these products, and you will find many other shops in the shopping malls. The suqs, for example the Kuwaiti suq, sell the cheaper brands.

Bugshan	464 8926
Gazzaz	462 6688
Saudi House	465 3515
Fitaihi	478 2012

Photographic Equipment and Processing   The best places to have your print and slide films processed in Riyadh are Shamsan Stores (T), at al-Akariya Olaya and al-Azizia Road on Exit 9, and Samir Photographic (T) in Olaya Road next to the Port Store and in the al-Jazeerah Supermarket Mall. Samir processes slides and Shamsan has a machine for making instant print copies of slides. MEPPS (T), opposite Circle supermarket in Thalateen Sulaimaniya Street, also processes black and white film.

Shamsan Stores	463 1476
Samir Photo.	465 1453
MEPPS	465 0591

These are also good shops in which to purchase cameras, Shamsan is the agent for Pentax and Olympus cameras and operates a repair shop (T) for these cameras in the building next to al-Mousa Mall. Cheaper cameras may be found in the small shops selling electronic goods at the beginning of

Ba'tha Street, underneath and opposite the Ba'tha Hotel. In this area there are many small shops selling electronic goods.

Passport photos or photos for identification purposes can be taken at Studio Nissah, next to the French Corner, Sara photo on al-Ahsa next to Safeway and GNC, or in one of the small photographic studios in Thalateen Sulaimaniya Street.

Shoes   Good shoe shops abound in Riyadh, especially on Olaya Road. For men's shoes try Bally at the junction of Olaya and Tahlia, Florsheim shoes at al-Akariya Sitteen (T) and al-Mousa Mall (T), or Clarks at the main store in Oruba Plaza (T) or the branches at al-Azizah Takhassusi (T) or al-Akariya Olaya (T). For women Milano sells good Italian shoes in the al-Nemer Centre opposite al-Akariya Olaya. Shoe Palace (T) at the corner of Olaya and Aruba streets has a wide range of expensive shoes while Shoe Mart (T), opposite Oruba Mall on King Fahad Expressway, has a cheaper selection of women's and children's shoes. Sports Kingdom (T) down Nosayr Street from al-Akariya mall has a large selection of sports shoes and hiking boots. Many small shops in the shopping malls and suq areas sell shoes and the major sports shops (Sports Ghornatah and Al-Faleh) stock running and aerobic shoes. Puma (T) on Olaya Road sell their branded shoes as well as sports equipment and clothes. For those with foot problems, Birkenstock Orthopedic Footwear (T) in the al-Mousa Mall, Shop #60, is well worth a visit.

Smoking   Cigarettes can be purchased very cheaply in supermarkets or small shops everywhere. Cigars are particularly good at Le Gourmet (T), on Thalateen Olaya Street. The *shisha,* or hubble-bubble pipes, are sold in the suqs (*see under* Suqs, page 32) or in several shops in Thalateen Olaya Street. Here you can also buy the mixtures smoked in these pipes, and all the bits and pieces necessary for the serious *shisha* smoker.

Sports Equipment   The main stores for sports are Ghornatah (T) on King Fahad Expressway and al-Faleh Sports Store (T) on Sitteen Road. These two chain stores stock equipment, sports clothing and shoes, and exercise machines; they have additional outlets in major malls and elsewhere in the

Florsheim	
Al-Akariya	462 3124
Al-Mousa	478 9737
Clarks	
Oruba Plaza	419 2521
Takhasusi	488 2593
Olaya	460 1308
Shoe Mart	419 2097
Sports Kingdom	462 4601
Puma	465 0477
Birkenstock	462 7801
Le Gourmet	465 4737
Ghornatah	465 2064
Al-Faleh Sports	477 0505

A golf course near Riyadh

city. Golf clothing and equipment can be found at ProGolf (T) on King Abdulaziz Road opposite the White Palace Hotel or at one of the pro shops at the Arizona compound driving range, the Dirab Golf Course, or the Inter-Continental Hotel Golf Course (*See* Sports p 75). Skin diving and Scuba equipment are sold by Red Sea Divers (T) on Olaya Road between Oruba Road and Kuwaiti suq, Durrah Dive Centre (T), around the corner from the al-Jazeerah Superstore, and Sea and Sun (T) on Sulaimaniya Thalateen Road between the Safeway and Old Airport.

ProGolf	479 3872
Red Sea Divers	464 4134
Durrah Dive Cent.	464 4134
Sea & Sun	479 2550

Toiletries   You can find most essentials in any supermarket or pharmacy. There are branches of Body Shop (T) and Body Reform (T) in al-Akariya centre, Olaya, and elsewhere, selling healthy products for the body and bathroom which have not been tested on animals.

Body Shop	463 3502
Body Reform	463 0265

Toys and Gifts for Children   Jarir Bookshop (T), branches on Olaya Road and on al-Ahsa (Pepsi) Road, sells a good range of children's toys, including bicycles and climbing equipment, and children are welcome to try out some of the bigger games. Toys R Us (T) and Toyland (T) on King Fahad Expressway have wide selections of toys, and children are welcome to try out some of the bigger items. Early Learning Centre (T) by the al-Nemer Centre and al-Azizia Takhassusi (T) has excellent educational toys, including puzzles and craft kits. Kuwaiti suq has a range of shops selling cheap toys and games; *see* Suqs, page 34.

For children's parties, you can buy balloons in many places in Riyadh and have them printed with the wording or design of your choice. The Good Ship Lollipop (T), on Tahlia Street near its junction with Olaya Road, is a good source – and also offers a complete party service – as is Bayt al-Balloon (T) near Jazeerah supermarket. Occasions (T), on Olaya Road by al-Akariya shopping centre, Olaya, is good for all things needed for a children's party.

Jarir Bookshop	462 6000
Toys R Us	419 5555
Toyland	464 8312
Early Learning Centre	
Al-Nemer	462 4695
Al-Aziziah	480 3461
Good Ship Lollipop	462 4064
Bayt al-Baloon	464 3996
Occasions	464 1545

Videos   Videos of current and classic films are available for sale at counters or small shops at most of the major supermarkets. A larger selection can be found at al-Baljoon (T), opposite the Chamber of Commerce on Dabbab Street. Video Channel 3 (T) on al-Hamdan Street, close to al-Jazeerah Superstore, both rents and sells English and American video cassettes. A membership of SR150 includes one week rental of three videos; subsequent rentals costs SR10 per video per week. All video cassettes for sale or rental in Saudi Arabia have been censored.

Al-Baljoon	404 1421
Video Channel 3	465 1955

Services

Barbers and Hairdressers   The hotels are excellent places in which men may have their hair cut, especially the Marriott (T)

Marriott	477 9300
Hyatt Regency	479 1234

Hyatt Regency	479 1234
Al-Khozama	465 4650
Inter-Continental	465 5000
French Corner	464 5333

and Hyatt Regency (T).

Most large compounds offer beauty services, such as facials and hairdressing. As turnover of compound residents and employees is rapid, personal recommendation is your best resource. If you see someone with fabulous hair, ask where she had her hair done (and hope it wasn't Paris!)

Catering

Most hotels, particularly the al-Khozama (T), the Inter-Continental (T) and the Hyatt Regency (T) have a good catering service. The European-trained chefs, eager to display their culinary skills, will work closely with you to design a dinner to your specifications. Not only food, but also tables, chairs, china, cutlery and glasses can be supplied for worry-free entertainment. The al-Khozama (T) and Inter-Continental Hotel (T) are to be recommended, as is the Hyatt Regency (T) where the chef, at the time of writing, is German. French Corner (T), where the chef is, of course, French, has an excellent catering service for parties of all sizes, or they will supply just one dish, such as a large stuffed fish or a cake.

For party-style cakes or gâteaux, the patisseries on Thalateen Olaya Street have wonderful confections, as does French Corner (T).

For children's parties *see* Lollipop and Bayt al-Baloon, p47.

Dry-cleaners

Dry-cleaning is relatively cheap in Riyadh but some of the small places offering this service are unreliable. For

The Hyatt Regency hotel

clothes you care about, you will probably find the dry-cleaning service offered by the supermarkets, and hotels, particularly the Hyatt Regency (T) and the Marriott Hotel (T) service at the Marriott workers' compound close to the junction of Exit 15 and Powerline Roads, the most reliable places to have good clothes dry-cleaned. Express dry-cleaning is done by several shops in Thalateen Sulaimaniya Street.

Hyatt Regency	479 1234
Marriott	477 9300

Movers and Packers
Four Winds (T), Namma Cargo Services (T), and Camel Inc. (T) can all be recommended. DHL (T) will supply a "jumbo box" for express cargo service.

Four Winds	454 4080
Namma Cargo	465 4200
Camel Inc	454 6572
DHL	462 1919

Painting and Decorating
Jotun Paints (T) on Takhassusi Street, near Azizia supermarket, will mix paints to match any colour you choose.

Jotun	446 8282

Printers
There are a number of good printing offices for stationery, cards and so on such as Hala Printing Press (T), on the Dammam/Makkah Highway, and Samha Press (T), off Aruba Road. Alphagraphics (T) just off the intersection of Olaya and Khorais Roads offers one stop copy shop and colour printing services including logo or brochure design and computer input.

Hala Printing	482 9620
Samha Press	465 8976
Alphagraphics	464 1600

Tailors, Dressmakers and Handicrafts
There are many cheap and good tailors and dressmakers in Riyadh. If women wish to be fitted, they must go to a "women only" dressmaker, such as the ones on the same street as Hammadi Hospital. Almost any tailor will copy an item of clothing brought to him or will tailor something from a sketch or magazine illustration if given the individual's measurements. Al-Akariya Ladies Tailoring (T) and Saysan Ladies Tailoring (T) near al-Akariya Olaya are well-known as efficient copiers of clothing. Al-Jalabiya, shop #393 in the al-Shola Shopping Centre, transforms the glittering silver-threaded Kashmiri shawls into evening jackets and vests and also copies clothing. Another tailor patronised by the expatriate community is al-Ghadir Fashion (T) marked with the blue and white awning on the street that intersects with Thalateen Olaya at the Panda supermarket.

Al-Akariya	465 6698
Saysan Ladies Tailoring	465 5481
Al-Ghadir Fashion	464 7663
House of Talents	465 9073
ADEL	464 5878

Men can also find good tailoring shops, in particular on Thalateen Olaya Street and between Panda on Thalateen Olaya and Can Restaurant on Tahlia Street.

An excellent Korean tailor is located on King Fahad Expressway immediately before al-Faisaliyah Tower.

House of Talents (T) and ADEL (signed in Arabic only), both opposite al-Akariya Olaya shopping centre in the

Circon Building, have a wide range of sewing and handi-craft supplies and, importantly for the handicraft maker, will obtain things you need if they are not in stock.

Upholstery and Furnishings

Dewaish	479 4311
Jazirah Furnishing	463 2361
Beity	465 5449

Dewaish (T), behind the Royal Commission for Yanbu and Jubail on al-Ahsa (Pepsi) Road, Jazirah Furnishing and Decoration Co. (T), in the al-Saif building diagonally opposite Can Restaurant, and Beity (T) on Tahlia Street, will all cover furniture in material either bought from them or supplied by you.

Transport and Travel

Travel Letters

When you are travelling outside the city of Riyadh, by plane or by car, you should carry a travel letter in Arabic from your sponsor, giving you permission to travel to specified areas and towns. There are checkpoints outside every town where the driver must stop and may be asked to show his *iqama* (identity card) and, occasionally, travel letter. Women travelling around the Kingdom outside Riyadh without their husbands need to carry a letter from their husbands giving them permission to do so.

Hukm *or Governorate*

Buses

There are two sorts of buses operating in Riyadh, neither really suitable for expatriate women. The buses run by the government-owned company SAPTCO are white with orange or blue stripes, while the private buses may be any colour. Both run along many different routes, such as the very busy Manfouhah to Old Airport route, which runs along

Ba'tha Street and up King Abdulaziz Street (Old Airport Road). The standard rate at the time of writing is SR2 for any distance.

Taxis or Limousines
Taxis (limousines) abound and can be hailed on any major road. Payment is very reasonable and is by meter. Always check the meter is activated as you enter the limo: the price starts at SR5. An acceptable price from King Khaled Airport to the city centre would be between SR40 and SR50. Women should always sit in the back of limousines. Most drivers speak some English.

At the airport there is also another type of taxi, the yellow Saudi taxi, where the price is fixed by negotiation, while the limousine fare is pre-determined, depending on your destination.

You can telephone for a limousine, if you are able to explain to the company where you live. Some limousine companies, such as Hala, will keep a map to your house on file, and will send you a regular driver if you so request. The following numbers may be helpful:

Hala Limousine, with branches at Sulaimaniya, near Old Airport (T), al-Akariya shopping centre (T), and at the Eye Hospital (which is the nearest office to the Diplomatic Quarter) (T). There is also Shary Limousine (T), behind Military Hospital, Sulaimaniyah, and Saudi Limousine (T).

Hala Limousine	
Sulaimaniya	463 3529
Al-Akariya	465 1451
Eye Hospital	482 1234
	Ext.1262
Shary Limousine	477 7313
Saudi Limousine	463 1416

The Nasiriyah Gate

Driving Licence
Only men may drive in Saudi Arabia. Visitors or those on a visit visa may use their own country's licence for the duration of their visit, but those on residence visas must obtain a Saudi licence (unless they are from GCC countries, in which case their own licence is valid in Saudi Arabia). For some nationals it will be necessary to take a driving test; for others, includ-

ing American, British and most European nationals, the licence of their country will exempt them from this necessity. Everyone, however, is required to take an eye test and a blood test at an approved local clinic or hospital.

Obtaining a new driving licence is a complicated process and in most cases will be dealt with by a local representative of your employer or sponsor. If you have to do it yourself, allow plenty of time. The office for licences, including renewals and testing, is at Dallah, just off Takhassusi Street on the left, shortly before Takhassusi joins the Ring Road North. As it is difficult to turn left on Takhassusi, it is better to approach from the Ring Road, exit 3. The turning to the Dallah office is not marked by a sign at the time of writing, but lies almost opposite the petrol station of Saad al-Faraaj, and is the end of the run for all number 9 buses, so there are plenty of buses to help you locate the place.

You can renew a driving licence at the Dallah centre or at any station of the traffic police (*murur*). The main traffic police station is in Nasiriyah, the next biggest is in Malaaz, opposite the Security Forces Hospital just off Sitteen Street, and there is one in King Abdulaziz Street (Old Airport Road).

Buying a Car

It is important to buy a vehicle with an efficient Riyadh-based service operation and immediate availability of spare parts. If you intend to do any serious, off-road, desert driving, a four-wheel-drive vehicle is essential. Used cars can be bought in the car suq, but you will need both considerable knowledge of cars and the stamina to rise above the noise and speed of bargaining. The supermarket notice boards are often a good source of information about second-hand cars for sale from private car owners.

The documentation process for new cars is complicated and must be carried out through the registered dealer. The vehicle has to be left with the dealer while the documentation is being processed. When a car is bought or sold, or

The King Faisal Foundation Centre

when the car registration book (*istamara*) is altered, it is necessary to acquire a MVPI (motor vehicle periodic inspection) certificate from the office clearly marked 'MVPI' by exit 8 of the Ring Road. This is equivalent to the annual inspections of vehicles demanded in other countries.

When driving around the city, you should keep the *istamara* in the car at all times. If you permit someone else to drive your car, it will be necessary for him to carry a letter from you giving him your permission in writing.

If you are stopped for a traffic violation, the traffic policeman will write down your *iqama* number when he gives you your ticket and the amount of the fine to be paid at the local Traffic Office. If the fine is not paid, the information will be entered into the airport computer system and you will not be allowed to leave the Kingdom.

Spare Parts

These are best obtained through the dealer from whom you buy your car. A wide variety of car parts and accessories are available from Rail Street, where you will also find a good selection of tools of all kinds. Tyres and some other car parts need to be changed more often in Saudi Arabia than in other countries because of the heat.

Car Hire

This is relatively cheap and is widely available in Riyadh. There are a number of car-hire offices at the airport, on the Dammam Highway by the Pepsi roundabout and near the old airport. There is one car-hire firm, Arab Motors (T) on the Dammam/Makkah Highway, which rents four-wheel drive vehicles, essential if you plan to do any off-road desert driving.

Arab Motors	233 2222

It is usually necessary to leave a signed credit card payment slip as a deposit when you hire a car.

Driving Manners and Customs

Newcomers to Saudi Arabia will be surprised to find that inexperienced drivers, intending to turn left at intersections, sometimes cut across the advancing traffic from the inside lanes – the cause of many accidents. Lane discipline is not strictly adhered to. Caution is always advisable at intersections, especially unfrequented ones, as the inattentive sometimes disdain STOP signs.

Roundabout (circle) code is to give way to traffic already circulating. Saudi Arabia operates a four-way traffic light system at crossroads, but allows drivers to filter into a right turn in the kerb-side lane against a red light. However, care should be taken in this manoeuvre since drivers doing this do not have priority.

There is little inhibition about overtaking on the inside lane and therefore it is necessary to keep a close eye on your rear-view mirrors! Slip-roads are sometimes deceptively broad and

ACS   482 9604

can be mistaken for the main highway. If you take one, you may be forced to make an unwanted right turn.

Desert driving courses are held from time to time: ask American Community Services (ACS) (T).

Accidents
In the event of a road accident, do not move your vehicle until the police advise you that you may, and wait by your vehicle. If your company has a government relations official, he should if possible be summoned to the scene of the accident. If there are injuries, summon an ambulance by dialling 997, if you can reach a phone. The police should also be summoned by dialling 999. When someone has been injured, all parties, irrespective of culpability, may be subject to temporary arrest.

Train Travel
Saudi Arabia's train runs from Riyadh to Dammam, stopping at Hofuf, and is a very pleasant way to travel. There are family coaches for women and children, and women accompanied by their husbands. The trains are clean, air-conditioned and smooth-running and have mobile snack trolleys. Riyadh station, with its huge and splendid brass globe lights, is situated in the old industrial estate, the Sinaiya. Tickets should be purchased at the station the day before you travel, and are very reasonably priced: first class SR60 to Dammam, SR45 to Hofuf (one way), second class SR40 to Dammam and SR30 to Hofuf (one way), at the time of writing. The journey from Riyadh to Dammam takes four hours.

Coaches
There are long-distance coaches operating to Taif, Makkah, Dammam, Hofuf, Buraida and Medina, run by the government-owned company SAPTCO. These also cross the border into Jordan and Syria. The depot is in front of the Ba'tha Hotel on Ba'tha.

Air Travel
The following airlines operate into and out of Riyadh: the national carrier Saudi Arabian Airlines and Air France, Air India, Air Lanka, Biman, British Airways, Cyprus Airways, Egypt Air, Emirates, Gulf Air, Middle East Airline, Olympic Airways, Pakistan International, Philippine Air, Swissair, Syrian Air, Turkish Air, TWA, Yemenia. Tickets can be purchased at the airline offices (telephone numbers and locations at the back of the book). There are also many reputable travel

Kanoo Travel   477 2228

Attar Travel   478 7208

Al-Tayyar
Travel Centre   463 3133

agencies which not only sell airline tickets but also make other travel arrangements, such as car and hotel reservations, and offer a variety of package and individual tours. Kanoo Travel (T) has several branches, including one on King Abdulaziz Street (Old Airport Road). Attar Travel (T) is off the Dammam Makkah Highway between Sitteen and al-Ahsa Road; al-

Tayyar Travel Centre (T) is on King Fahad Expressway.

Boarding passes for Saudi Arabian Airlines flghts can be picked up 24 hours in advance of departure at the Saudi Arabian Airlines office, just off the King Fahad Expressway past the Riyadh Exhibition Hall.

Be warned that there is serious pressure of space on domestic and international flights at the Haj season and at other holiday periods. On Saudia flights you need to re-confirm your flight some 72 hours before departure. You can check on flight arrivals and departures by ringing King Khaled Airport direct (T).

King Khaled Airport Info	220 2968

Hotels and Restaurants

Hotels

Riyadh has excellent, reasonably-priced hotels. Most have sports facilities for guests and non-guests (*see* Sports, page 75). All hotels have restaurants, open to both residents and others, with family sections where women can enjoy lunch or dinner. Many hotels host a Friday brunch, which is popular with families as special activities are often offered for the children, and feature the food of different nationalities on a rotating evening schedule. The four- and five-star hotels have excellent chefs, many trained in Europe, who lavish their culinary expertise on everything from appetizers to desserts. Eating out is a pleasure in Riyadh with a variety of food festivals celebrating everything from game to asparagus at different seasons of the year. If you have a yearning for a certain type of cuisine, the hotels often do a round-robin of ethnic cuisines during the week, assigning each evening to a particular region's specialities.

Five-star Hotels:
Hyatt Regency (T)
Inter-Continental Hotel (T), near the Ministry of the Interior.
Riyadh Marriott Hotel (T), Ma'ather Street.
Sahara Hotel (T), near the airport.
Al-Faisaliyah (T) (open April 2000)
Olaya Holiday Inn (T)

Hyatt Regency	479 1234
Inter-Continental	465 5000
Marriott	477 9300
Sahara	220 4500
Al-Faisaliyah	464 4650
Olaya Holiday Inn	461 2000

Four-star
Al-Khozama Hotel (T), on Olaya Road.
Minhal Holiday Inn (T), on King Abdulaziz Street (Old Airport Road).
Riyadh Sheraton (T), on the junction of King Fahad Street and the road leading to the University.
Riyadh Palace (T).
Al-Mutlaq Novotel (T), on King Abdulaziz Street (Old Airport Road), near the old airport.

Al-Khozama	465 4650
Minhal Holiday Inn	478 2500
Sheraton	454 3300
Riyadh Palace	405 4444
Al-Mutlaq Novotel	476 0000

Restaurants
The following are recommended:

Saudi

Nejd Village	464 6530
Shaabiyah	419 8581
Al-Nakheel	465 4650

▸ *Nejd Village* (T) on Takhassusi Street offers a Saudi dining experience, including baby camel. Phone ahead for the famiIy dining schedule.
▸ *Shaabiyah* (T), on Olaya road just north of Aruba Street, serves excellent Saudi cuisine in the traditional setting of a tent, with seating on a carpet outside or inside, and also does take-away.
▸ *The al-Nakheel Restaurant* (T) at the top of the al-Khozama Towers often includes a Saudi dish, along with Moroccan and Tunisian specialities, in its Arabian buffet.

American

Steak House	464 9638
Ferdaus	477 3900

▸ *The Steak House* (T) on Thalateen Olaya Street opposite Panda supermarket has excellent steaks.
▸ *The Ferdaus Steakhouse* at the Marriot Hotel specialises in American steaks with all the trimmings in a Southwestern atmosphere.

Lebanese/Syrian

Bourj al-Hammam	
Old Airport Rd	441 1401
Aruba St	465 7686
Baalbek	464 1154
Yamal Asham	461 3293
Al-Madareb	465 7361
Al-Ajami	464 3865
Panorama	220 4500

▸ *Bourj al-Hammam,* Takhassusi Street, near King Faisal Specialist Hospital (T), and Aruba Street, (T), good take-away.
▸ *Baalbek Restaurant* (T), Aruba Street, good take-away.
▸ *Yamal Asham* on Old Airport Road (men only) and Olaya Street (with an outdoor patio area and family section) offers a wide range of Lebanese food and one of the best *shwarma* in Riyadh.
▸ *Al-Madareb* (T) on Dabbab Road serves Lebanese and Syrian food with a little atmosphere: old guns hang on the walls of the men's section and woven tent hangings act as dividers in the family section.
▸ *Al-Ajami* (T) on Thalateen Olaya is a men only restaurant, but women can order and take away dinners.
▸ *The al-Rabeea* chain of restaurants, located in many parts of the city, supplies *mezze*, Lebanese hors d'oeuvres, to many Saudi homes and does excellent kebabs and *shish taouk* (marinated chicken cubes) for take out.
▸ For an Arab ending to a meal, visit the *Panorama* restaurant on the roof of the Sahara Airport Hotel and smoke a *narghile* in a tapestry tent.

French

Café Can	465 8007
L'Ecluse	465 7648
French Corner	464 5322

▸ *Café Can* (T), on Tahlia Street does take-away and outside catering.
▸ *L'Ecluse* (T) on Tahlia Street
▸ *French Corner* (T), Dabbab Street, also sells excellent bread and pastries and does outside catering (ring the chef for details).

Japanese
- *Furusato* (T), on Tahlia Street
- *Tokyo Restaurant* (T), on Arubah Road, take-away.
- *Shogun* (T), Hyatt Regency, King Abdulaziz Street (Old Airport Road).

Italian
- *Da Pino* (T), 1st floor, al-Khozama centre, Olaya Road.
- *Roma,* (T) off Olaya Road, near al-Akariya centre.

Mexican
- *Mexican Connection* (T), Sulaimaniya, outside catering.

Chinese
- *Golden Dragon* (T) opposite al-Akariya Olaya.
- *Jade Garden* (T), off King Abdulaziz Street (Old Airport Road), has a Mongolian barbecue, and does take-away and outside catering.
- *Gulf Royal* (T), Olaya Road, take-away, outside catering.
- *Memories of China* (T), between Olaya Road and King Fahad Highway.

Thai
- *Bangkok Seafood Restaurant* (T) in the Circon Building opposite al-Akariya shopping centre, Olaya.

Turkish
- There are a large number of very reasonable Turkish restaurants, such as *Assaraya Turkish Restaurant* (T), in Thalateen Olaya Street, which does take-away meals.

Indian and Pakistani
- *Marhaba Restaurant* (T), Olaya Road, take-away.
- *Wajbah* (T), opposite FAL shopping centre, on King Abdulaziz Street (Old Airport Road), take-away.
- *La Sani* (T) behind the al-Nemer Centre on Olaya.
- *Dum Pukht* (T) on Tahlia Street
- *Shezan Indian Restaurant* (T), King Fahad Road.

Furusato	465 7648
Tokyo	464 5672
Shogun	479 1234
Da Pino	465 4650
Roma	464 1133
Mexican Conn	450 9575
Golden Dragon	462 7168
Jade Garden	465 0825
Gulf Royal	463 1622
Memories of China	462 6609
Bangkok Seafood	465 1416
Assaraya	464 9336
Marhaba	462 2070
Wajbah	453 1086
La Sani	465 5666
Dum Pukht	465 4109
Shezan	462 6608

NOTE THAT RESTAURANTS ARE CLOSED DURING PRAYER TIME.

In addition to the take-away service offered by the above, there are plenty of small take-away suppliers, especially of Turkish and Lebanese food and pizzas. To find a useful little square containing many small restaurants with take-away facilities, go past Aziziah supermarket along Takhassusi Road, leaving Aziziah on your left. At the first lights, turn right, and you will find the square on your right some 300 metres along, opposite a small mosque. Men might find the restaurant Yamal Asham on King Abdulaziz

Street (Old Airport Road) useful for a quick snack of sandwich or *shwarma*, or something more substantial, which can be eaten there or taken away. The Yamal Asham on Olaya Street close to Jarir bookstore has family dining with waiter service upstairs as well as open-air dining for men downstairs The Syrian al-Burj (T), on Thalateen Sulaimaniya Street near its junction with King Abdulaziz Street, sells delicious slipper-shaped sandwiches for SR2 and spicy bread (*za'atha*) for SR3 – excellent for picnics. Many of the local bakeries will serve bread coated with ghee and sugar, sprinkled with sesame seeds, and caramelised under the fire as a breakfast treat.

Al-Burj	462 0692

Fast-food restaurants have inundated the city. McDonald's, Wendy's, Hardees, Kentucky Fried Chicken, Long John Silver's, Herfy, Taco Bell, Pizza Hut, Pizza Italia, Pizza Inn, Big Boy, Kudu, Burger King, and Dairy Queen have outlets throughout the city. Dunkin' Donuts, TCBY, Baskin Robbins, and Heidi's Ice Cream are good places to stop with the children when shopping.

Many compounds have excellent restaurants and it is often possible for non-residents to use these, by prior arrangement. The Diplomatic Quarter has a rather charming piazza in the middle where it is possible to sit and sip a coffee or cold drink in the open air.

Libraries

King Abdulaziz Public Library	493 4708

King Abdulaziz Public Library (T), opposite the National Guard headquarters on the Dammam/Makkah Highway (turn right at the lights just before exit 13 of the Ring Road, by the College of Physical Education for Teachers), has a vast collection of books in Arabic, English, French and German for public use. In a cool, quiet atmosphere, students and others can browse through books and periodicals on a wide range of subjects, including

The King Abdulaziz Library

history, archaeology, geography, medicine, English literature and language and Arabic literature for foreign learners. The collection includes some rare, old manuscripts. Readers may take away photocopies of books held by the Library, or borrow them after leaving a substantial deposit.

Men may use the library daily, Saturday to Wednesday, from 8.00 am to 9.00 pm and on Thursdays from 8.00 am to 2.00 pm. Ladies gain access to the library through a separate entrance at the back of the building and may use the library from 8.00 am to 1.00 pm, Saturday to Wednesday, and 4.00 pm to 8.00 pm, Saturday to Tuesday. Children may attend special programmes, particularly during the Eid holidays, in a well-appointed children's library.

The King Fahd Library is open to non-Saudis, primarily scholars doing research in the Kingdom who have letters of request from their home universities, or who are in the Kingdom as Fulbright or other government-supported academic scholars. The library also hold all PhD dissertations, available for reading, by Saudi doctoral candidates at home and abroad.

King Faisal Foundation
Centre (fax)   465 9993

The King Faisal Foundation Centre (T) has a computerised library for use by individual students or groups. For groups an appointment must be made. Individuals may use the library as follows:

Women: Saturday to Wednesday, 4.00 pm-10.00 pm
Men: Saturday to Wednesday, 8.30 am-2 pm.

ACS   482 9604

American Community Services Library, (ACS) (T) down the *wadi* beneath the Diplomatic Quarter, has a good selection of adult and juvenile fiction and non-fiction books for borrowing, and reference and travel brochures can be used in the library itself. It is open to members as follows:

The King Fahad Library

Saturday, 9.00 am-4.00 pm
Sunday, 9.00 am-4.00 pm and 6.00 pm-9.00 pm
Monday 10.30 am-6.00 pm
Tuesday 9.00 am-4.00 pm
Wednesday 9.00 am-4.00 pm
Thursday 10.00 am-4.00 pm and 6.00 pm-9.00 pm
Membership of the ACS (which entitles you to use the library) is open to American citizens, or families in which one parent holds an American passport.
Membership for a fiscal year is SR175 for a family, SR125 for an individual.

Banks

There are ten banks in Riyadh in which an account may be opened. ATM machines are to be found all over the city – some are drive-in – and the ATM card of one bank can be used in any of the others.
Arab National Bank
Al Fransi Bank
Al Jazirah Bank
National Commercial Bank (NCB)
Al Rajhi Bank
Riyadh Bank
Saudi American Bank
Saudi British Bank
Saudi Hollandi Bank
Saudi Investment Bank
Opening hours for most banks, excluding prayer times: 8.30 am-12.00 pm, 5.00-6.30 or 7.00 pm.
Women may use the ladies' branches of banks, which, in many cases, will be an annex to the men's branch, and in many cases can use the men's branches as well.

The Saudi Arabian Monetary Agency

Education

Nursery
There are private groups offering both play facilities and pre-school education to young children. For more details contact your embassy (*see* page 86, telephone numbers).

Primary and Secondary
There are a number of primary and secondary schools in Riyadh, for non-Saudi children up to the age of fourteen, under the aegis of the Ministry of Education. These form the Saudi-Arabian International Schools, Riyadh (SAIS). They follow approved national curricula and teach in the language of their country. The following schools form the SAIS group (*see* page 86 *et seq.*, telephone numbers).

    The American School (pre-kindergarten to 12 years)
    The British School (reception to year 9)
    The French School
    The German School
    The Japanese School

    There are other smaller private schools, which cater to the needs of children from some other national groups.

▸ *The Dutch School* (T), on the Kingdom City compound off Ring Road exit 5, accepts Dutch-speaking children between the ages of four and twelve. There is also a playground and nursery on the compound.

▸ *The Swedish School* (T), on the Philipps Ericsson compound, accepts children from Norway, Finland and Denmark as well as Sweden, from the ages of six to twelve (grades 1-6). The teaching is in Swedish.

Dutch School	275 0275
Swedish School	246 2400 Ext.2465

Multinational School	454 1686

4 *The Multinational School* (T) teaches an Australian curriculum in English but takes children of many different nationalities; it was founded in order to offer an educational programme to children with learning or physical disabilities.

Playground in the Science Oasis

Indian Embassy School	231 8092

4 *The Indian Embassy School* (T) is located on Khorais Road at the Rawadah 2 exit.

Many other schools cater to children of diferent nationalities. Every school should be licenced by the Ministry of Education. If it is not, it may be closed down in mid-year. Before enrolling children in any school, ask to see the Ministry of Education licence.

Adult Education

Courses for women A posting to Riyadh is a great opportunity to learn a new skill or language and there are plenty of places, private and public, where you can take courses in any number of subjects, such as art, handicrafts or bridge. In addition to the organisations listed below, ask your friends and national groups such as the American Community Services (T).

ACS	482 9604

4 *American Community Services,* which operates on American Embassy property, hosts a variety of women's and family events. American passport holders can become members by paying a fee and may then use the library and facilities. All non-Saudi passport holders as well as members may take advantage of the continuing educational opportunites in languages, computers, art, and physical exercise. ACS runs a summer camp and offers many volunteer opportunities, such as making crafts for the seasonal bazaars, organising childrens' activities, and working on special functions

Al-Nahda Philanthropic Society	464 9259

4 *Al-Nahda Philanthropic Society for Women* (T), based in Sulaimaniya, exists to develop and direct women's abilities and to organise local philanthropic activities. It runs courses for women in arts, computer skills and languages, holds bazaars and exhibitions, and looks after the needy, especially the handicapped, orphans and the poor. It also has a collection of antique dresses from different regions within the Kingdom and is working to preserve the traditions of dressmaking and embroidery by copying old designs in a modern workshop.

Courses offered by the Society, which are open to all nationalities, include:

Basic Islam

Languages: English, French, Italian, Arabic
Computing and word-processing
Cooking
Fashion and interior design
Fine Arts: drawing, watercolour painting, pottery
Courses for children

▶ *Al-Manahil Centre* (T), in the Diplomatic Quarter, run by and for women, offers a wide range of educational, cultural and recreational activities, holds exhibitions and has a restaurant. It is situated in the Diplomatic Quarter but women of all nationalities from all over the city use its facilities. Every week there is a ladies' dinner and a ladies' brunch featuring food from different parts of the world. For children, there are spring and summer camps, weekly parties, and recreational evenings with organised team sports. The courses for adults include: Quran, languages (English, Arabic, French and Spanish), computer skills, nutrition, cooking, dressmaking, jewellery design, batik, painting on glass, art history, collage, weaving, painting on silk, drawing, oil painting, skin care and hair styling, interior design, flower arrangement and calligraphy.

Al-Manahil Cent 482 9755

▶ *The Centre for Continuing Education* (T). The women's section of this branch of King Saud University is situated near the back entrance to the television station. Both Saudi and non-Saudi women can take courses here in Arabic, English, French or computing skills. The cost varies with the subject to be studied. The classes start in September each year and last from two to twelve weeks. The academic year is divided into two semesters.

Centre for Continuing
Education   402 4700

▶ *The Middle East Centre for Human Development* (T). Located in a villa behind Aruba Road (turn right at al-Shablan Pharmacy and then take the second left), this centre offers French language courses, following the Alliance Française programme, under the sponsorship of the French Embassy. Admission and placement is by examination and native speakers from France, Tunisia, and other countries teach all classes.

Middle East Centre for
Human Dev.   465 1505

▶ *The British Council* (T) runs English language programmes for women at the al-Manahil Centre in the Diplomatic Quarter. The University of Cambridge CELTA (Certificate in English Language Teaching to Adults) and DELTA (Diploma in English Language Teaching to Adults) both qualify teachers to work in English language training schools, including those of the British Council. With one of these credentials, it is also possible to find private tutoring work with university students and graduates in the Riyadh area.

British Council   480 7811
(courses at al-Manahil)

The British Council at its al-Mousa Mall office (T) offers information on long distance learning programmes offered to women by professional schools and universities in the United Kingdom. It also arranges for monitored examinations for the GCSE, professional, and graduate courses on request.

British Council
 Al-Mousa Mall 462 1818

Language Centre for Girls	464 9515
British Council	462 1818
European Centre for Languages and Training	476 1218
	476 4680/476 9698
Centre for Continuing Education	402 4700
Centre Saoudien	476 6436

▸ *The Language Centre for Girls* (T), in Dabbab Street, Sulaimaniya, near Forsan, offers courses in English, French, computing skills and typing. There are nine levels of English on offer, from basic to advanced.

Courses for Men The British Council (T), situated in the al-Mousa centre, Olaya Road, offers courses in English to men, from beginner to advanced levels. The Cambridge examinations in English are offered twice yearly. Women may take the examinations but not the classes.
Course fees:
    Saudis, SR1420 for a seven-week course (42 hours)
    Non-Saudis, SR 1520
    Times of courses: 9.30-11.30 am
                                2.45-5.00 pm
                                8.30-10.30 pm.

▸ *The European Centre for Languages and Training* (T), behind McDonald's in Sitteen Street, offers a good range of courses in English to men and, during the summer, to boys. It can provide tailor-made courses in other fields, too, such as banking and finance.

▸ *The Centre for Continuing Education* (T), a branch of King Saud University, has a section for men in Washem Street where evening classes in a wide range of subjects is offered to Saudis and non-Saudis. The teaching is in Arabic, but special classes can be arranged in which a subject can be taught in English. Arabic language classes are also given; again the teaching is in Arabic.

▸ *The Centre Saoudien* (T), under the sponsorship of the French Embassy, offers courses in French language for men.

Shaded walkway in the Riyadh Diplomatic Quarter

THINGS TO DO AND SEE IN RIYADH

The Desert

Undoubtedly one of the most enjoyable things to do when you are living in Riyadh is to explore the desert, which lies on your doorstep with all its variety of rocky cliffs, tree-covered valleys and rolling sand-dunes. Go out for a day's exploration or picnic or, if you feel more adventurous and have a suitable vehicle, venture further afield for an overnight camp under the stars. Some of the more popular treks and excursions which can be made in the environs of Riyadh or further afield are described in the author's *Desert Treks from Riyadh*.

Do follow basic safety precautions. Never go alone; always tell someone where you are going; take plenty of water, a hat, good lace-up shoes, a spare tyre, and a means of extricating your car from soft sand. If you break down, wait by your car for help. There is a Natural History Society which meets regularly in Riyadh to discuss subjects connected with the desert, such as birds, flowers and history. Ask old Riyadh hands for details.

Sightseeing and Spectator Sports

Dira Square

There are very few vestiges of the old walled city of Riyadh. In the central square, known as Dira, with its famous Clock Tower, the new Grand Mosque stands on the site of the old Grand Mosque and the Governorate is on the site of the old ruler's palace. Tumeiri Street, which leads up to this square, is the one surviving street from the Riyadh of a hundred years ago. Dira has been beautifully re-developed using local stone. From the square you can see the ancient Musmak fortress: nearby are the Antique suqs, which seldom fail to fascinate the visitor or newcomer to Riyadh.

Musmak Fortress

This is probably the oldest building in Riyadh, dating from 1865. You have a good view of it from Dira Square. Walk up to the massive door alongside the postern gate. In it you can detect the hole made by the spear of Abdulaziz's friend Ibn Jiluwi, when he was rushing the entrance with the future King to seize the fortress from the Rashidi Governor in January 1902. This famous coup marked the beginning of Saudi rule. Musmak therefore holds a place of special significance in the history of the present Kingdom.

It was built as a palace during the Second Saudi state in the mid-nineteenth century but was probably re-built in the 1890s to serve as a base for the Rashidi garrison and Governor. In the time of King Abdulaziz it served as an arsenal, jail and storehouse.

The fortress now houses an excellent permanent exhibition showing the history of the building, its dramatic capture by the future King Abdulaziz, his subsequent unification of the Kingdom, and the history of Riyadh itself. The exhibition has a fascinating selection of old photographs of Riyadh and other parts of the Kingdom, dating almost from the beginning of this century. There are maps and plans of the city of Riyadh, old and new, and four lively films showing re-enactments of aspects of history, such as the capture of the fortress. The exhibition is open to the public without prior arrangement or entrance fee and is well worth seeing.

above left: Restored room in the Musmak Fort
above right: The Musmak Fort

Fortress Opening times:
8.00 am-12.00 pm, 4.00-9.00 pm every weekday, closing only at prayer-times.

The King Abdul Aziz Historical Centre

The Historical Centre, opened in celebration of the Kingdom's Centenary, contains exhibition buildings, restored and renovated architectural heritage sites, green parks and open spaces, libraries and research centres which will become the cultural centre of Riyadh.

National Museum
402 9500 x 1082

▸ *The National Museum* (T) opened in January 1999 to acknowledge the 100th anniversary of the modern Saudi State, founded by Ibn Saud. The comprehensive exhibits cover the history of Saudi Arabia from neolithic times through the advent of Islam and the founding of the Saudi State. Audio-visual films depict the endangered species of Saudi Arabia and the variety of habitats and flora and fauna in the Kingdom. Separate exhibits examine the pre-Islamic culture of the Arabian Peninsula and the architecture of Medain Saleh, a centre of Nabatean civilisation. The Prophet's Mission Hall encapsulates what is known of the Prophet Mohammed's life while another exhibition details the founding and spread of Islam throughout the Arab world and beyond. Historical exhibitions discuss the First and Second Saudi States and the unification of the country under Ibn Saud. There is no better place to visit to get an overview of the dynamic changes in the life and culture of the Arabian Peninsula. A gift shop, to be opened in 2000, will sell copies of the national archaeological journal, al-Atlal, as well as souvenirs and books about Saudi Arabia.

The National Museum is the lynchpin of a cultural complex

The National Museum

including a number of other important institutions.

▸ *The Darat al-Malik Abdulaziz,* or King Abdulaziz Archives, researches and publishes historical documents about King Abdulaziz and the founding of the Saudi state. The Darat also manages the King Abdulaziz Memorial Hall which exhibits personal effects of the King and also hosts temporary exhibitions explaining the history of the Kingdom, A branch of the King Abdulaziz Public Library is open for women, men, and children. The children's section includes educational computer games as well as books. The Department of Antiquities, which gives permissions for archaeolical visits to Medain Salah and Qaryat al-Fau, is located in the two-story building next to the Museum.

▸ The restored *Murabba Palace* lies at one end of the pedestrian walkway and park tying the buildings together. Murabba is the remnant of the great administrative palace built in 1936 by King Abdulaziz, when the palace within the original city walls was no longer able to contain his increased household and administrative staff. The Murabba lay about a mile north of the old walled city of Riyadh and, with its great long walls intercepted with square towers, looked much like a town itself. When the King moved into this new palace in 1938 it marked the beginning of the expansion of Riyadh town beyond the old walls.

Not much of the old walls of the palace remain but the buildings which do still stand are interesting, since they represent the transitional period between mud and concrete as building materials.

You enter the main two-storey building, which has rooms opening off a central courtyard, in the centre of which a palm tree has sprouted out of the old well. On the first floor is the royal suite of reception, or *majlis*, rooms and a few glass cases containing old costumes. From the roof you have an interesting view over the intricate maze of rooms and palaces built over a period of time to house the King's wives and sons.

Central courtyard of the Murabba Palace

In the late afternoon and evening and on weekends the long *maidan* or open walkway tying these buildings together is filled with families and children enjoying the grassy picnic areas, the open air hands-on science centre, and the coolness afforded by the splashing fountains. City children enjoy, in particular, the wide flat court where they can bicycle and roller blade.

The National Museum is open to men and schools from 9 am to 12 noon on Sunday, Monday, Wednesday, and Thursday and from 4.30 to 9 pm on Tuesday. Family hours are from 4.30 to 9 pm on Sunday, Monday, Wednesday, Thursday, and Friday. Tuesday mornings are open by reservation only and the Museum is closed to the public on Saturday. Hours change during Ramadan. An entry ticket to the National Museum is SR15. Murabba Palace and the King Abdulaziz Memorial Hall are open during the same hours and entry is free.

Dir'iyyah

The old ruined capital of the al-Saud, dating from the sixteenth century but with its heyday in the eighteenth and early nineteenth centuries, lies just outside the city. The outer walls and certain key structures, including Prince Sa'ad's palace and the bath house, have been meticulously restored. Strolling through the abandoned alleys on a weekday afternoon, when few others are present, can vividly bring to mind the Saudi way of life as it was 200 years ago.

Dir'iyyah can be reached within half an hour from central Riyadh. No permission is necessary and no entrance fee is charged. *Dir'iyyah and the First Saudi State* by William Facey, published by Stacey International, gives an excellent history and description of the site.

Outside the ruined city, about 250 metres down the wadi from the right of the main entrance as you stand with your back to it, is an old, restored well which operates every day between 4.00 and 6.00 pm on payment of a few rials to the custodian. This is an interesting way of seeing how a traditional well worked by donkey power operates. The donkeys walk down a ramp dragging ropes attached to bags, which draw water up and over a palm beam, so that the water is poured into irrigation channels.

Janadriyah Festival and Camel Races
Every spring, usually the last week of March and the first of April, camel races are staged under the sponsorship of the National Guard on the Thumamah Road north out of Riyadh (Route 550). Racing beasts and their young cameleers gather from far and wide. The races are a prominent feature of the Riyadh year and are quite exciting to watch – there is no betting. The races are followed by a week-long cultural festival at which local crafts and handicrafts are displayed and sometimes sold, in a setting rather like an outdoor museum, with examples of different styles of Saudi architecture from all the regions of the Kingdom. There are separate days for men and for women to visit both the races and the festival. One day of the festival is reserved for family visits when parents can take their children and explain Saudi history and culture to them. Several days, during which the exhibits are staffed by women, are reserved for women only.

Traditional sword dance (**a'ardha**) *at Janadriyah National Heritage Fesitval*

Horse Races

The race-track at the end of Sitteen Street, by the Equestrian Club, has races every half hour on Sunday afternoons between 2.00 and 5.00 pm. There is a family section. No booking is necessary and no betting is permitted.

Natural History and Science

The Zoo

The Riyadh zoological gardens contain ibex, oryx and other species of animals, mainly indigenous to the Middle East but with some African and Far Eastern specimens as well. The animal pens and enclosures are very attractively laid out and maintained, and the flowering shrubs along walkways between the enclosures make this a pleasant place for a visit.

Men and women are not permitted to visit the zoo together.

A ring-tailed lemur in Riyadh Zoo

Women's days are Sundays, Tuesdays and Thursdays. Men's days are Mondays, Wednesdays and Fridays. On Saturdays the zoo is closed.

Opening times:
  Weekdays: 9.00 am-1.00 pm; 4.00 pm-nightfall
  Fridays: 4.00 pm-nightfall

Entrance fee:
  Children, SR3
  Adults, SR5

The Science Oasis

Within the Diplomatic Quarter there is an absorbing 'hands-on' museum, set up under the auspices of the Arriyadh Development Authority, in which basic scientific principles are demonstrated to children of all ages by encouraging them to learn by participation. The themes of the museum are astronomy, physics, mechanics and life sciences. There are

Science display in the Science Oasis

regular demonstrations in the planetarium and using the Van der Graaf static electricity generator. The museum has a powerful telescope with which members of the public can view the stars on scheduled evenings.

Opening times:

4.00-8.00 pm Sundays to Fridays (the museum is closed on Saturdays); Tuesday: men only.

School groups and organised tours: 9.00 am-4.00 pm Group reservations can be made (T).

Science Oasis
Reservations   482 8276

The National Commission for Wildlife Conservation and Development (NCWCD) Visitor Centre

The NCWCD, (near the Shumaisy hospital, opposite the Red Crescent), has a permanent exhibition of native wildlife. This includes stuffed oryx, ostrich and gazelle, models of dugong and sharks, and a salt-water aquarium containing examples of the species found among the coral off Arabian shores. There are demonstrations of the damage humans can cause to the environment. This small natural history museum is particularly interesting to children, and groups of school-children are regularly shown round.

Opening times: 8.00 am-2.00 pm Saturday to Wednesday

Groups: Apply in writing or by telephone or fax (T) to:

Dr. Abuzinada
Secretary-General, NCWCD
PO Box 61681
Riyadh 11575

NCWCD
tel: 441 0369
fax   441 0797

An Arabian oryx

The King Khalid Wildlife Research Centre

Within easy reach of Riyadh to the north, the Thumamah Research Centre (T), run by the NCWCD, has a research and breeding programme for indigenous, especially endangered, animal species, or those already extinct in the wild. Some animals raised in captivity, particularly gazelle, have already been re-introduced into the wild, and more releases are planned. The centre can be visited by appointment. Apply to The Secretary General, NCWCD.

Application by fax is usually the quickest way of obtaining this permission and should just take a day or two.

The King Faisal Centre for Research and Islamic Studies

The King Faisal Foundation, established in 1976, has as its objective the encouragement of scientific research and of cultural activities relating to all aspects of Islam. Awards are made annually for outstanding achievements in various fields of science and the arts.

The Centre was founded in 1983 to provide accessible resources for all kinds of academic research. There are collections of books, manuscripts and other Islamic works, some very rare. The main library is designed to accommodate a million books which can be accessed by computer. The manuscript library has an extensive collection of original hand-written volumes which can be studied by researchers and scholars, all of which have been placed on microfilm. Documents in poor condition are restored and preserved using the most up-to-date techniques. There is also a very attractive children's library.

The Centre can be visited by arrangement, usually by groups rather than individuals.
Apply (fax) to:
Yahya Bin Junaid
Director General
King Faisal Research Centre
PO Box 51049
Riyadh 11543
Tel: 461 3982
Fax: 465 9993
Opening times:
Men: Saturday to Wednesday 8.30 am-2.00 pm and 4.00 pm-10.00 pm
Women: Saturday to Wednesday, 4.00 pm-10.00 pm, in a separate section for women only.

There is also a museum (T) dedicated to the life of King Faisal and this may be visited without prior permission from 9.00 am-12.00 noon and 5.00 pm-9.00 pm. Mondays and Thursdays are reserved for families and for women.

Off the upstairs plaza there is another small museum which hosts a changing roster of temporary exhibits, primarily of Middle Eastern manuscripts and artifacts.

Thumamah Research Centre	
tel:	482 4983
fax:	441 0797

King Faisal Centre	
Museum	465 2255
	x 6400

Parks

Riyadh is scattered with small parks, some for men, others for families. Some of the bigger ones include:

The Diplomatic Quarter   This has something for every member of the family, with its lovely perimeter walk overlooking the Wadi Hanifah, its well-designed playgrounds scattered about the perimeter and, in the centre, its open piazza where families gather at weekends: here you will see parents drinking coffee at an outside café while the children roller-skate or skate-board around the paved area. Cycling is possible within or around the Diplomatic Quarter. The Arriyadh Development Authority, which has responsibility for the Diplomatic Quarter, has made a special effort to incorporate native plantings into its gardens. Use the gardens as a source of ideas for your own yard or garden.

A garden walk in the Diplomatic Quarter

Olaya Park   This is a cool, flowery refuge on a hot day, with a playground for children. It is open every day except Saturday, from 4.00-11.00 pm Sundays to Wednesdays, and from 2.00 pm to 12.00 am on Thursdays and Fridays. It is situated between the King Fahad Highway (turn right as you go south just before the fly-over connection with the Dammam/Makkah Highway) and the Dammam/Makkah Highway (behind the Haif Commercial Centre). Entrance fee SR5 per person.

Olaya Park

Malaaz Park   Located at the end of Sitteen Street on the left, this is a mature well-grown park with a few slides and other activities for children.

Durfa Park   This park is within the precincts of the old airport, and is approached by taking the road to the right as you face the old airport (now the Royal Saudi Airbase). It is open every day except Saturdays to women and children, from 4.00 pm to 11.00 pm on weekdays and from 2.00 pm to 11.00 pm at weekends. It costs SR2 for an adult, SR1 for a child. Here there are fewer trees and flowers than the parks already mentioned but perhaps more to do and it is very busy, particularly at weekends.

Camel's Eye Park   Near the Camel's Eye rock formation to the west of Sitteen Street, behind McDonald's, is an attractive park which is never open to women. Men and children may visit it every day except Thursday, between 4.00 pm and 12.00 noon. It costs SR2 for men, SR1 for children.

Camel's Eye Park

Al Foutah Park   To either side of the King Fahad Highway near the turn-offs to the suq areas are several kilometres of park-like small gardens with grass and trees, and slides and swings for children. These are free and open to all and are very much used.

Sports

There are plenty of sporting opportunities in Riyadh for men and women – you will soon find out about these by asking around or enquiring through your national organisations.

Private Sports
The larger compounds have swimming pools and tennis courts, and in some of these tennis leagues have been formed. Squash and badminton courts also exist. There are groups practising aerobics, callinetics, yoga and other such activities, as well as groups of runners. Scuba diving is very popular in the Arabian Gulf and the Red Sea and there are

Compound basketball court

two shops in Riyadh selling diving equipment (*see* page 47). Horse riding opportunities also exist – again you will have to ask around.

Public Sports and Clubs

All hotel sports clubs are open for men only. Memberships are offered for different time periods, ranging from one month to a year. Costs change often, so check with the individual hotels before making a decision based on facilities, location and price.

▸ *Sheraton Hotel Sports Club (T):*
Facilities: swimming, tennis, billiards, bowling, basketball, exercise room, sauna, steam-room.

Sheraton Hotel   454 3300

▸ *Inter-Continental Hotel Recreation and Sports Club (T):*
This club is located at Gate 12 behind the hotel.
Facilities: gym, steam-room, jacuzzi, tennis, squash, indoor and outdoor swimming.There is also a nine-hole golf course at the hotel (*see* page 76). The Inter-Continental also has a bowling alley, SR9 per game.

Inter-Continental 465 5000

▸ *Al-Khozama Hotel Sports Centre* (T):
This club is located on the first floor of the al-Khozama Centre.
Facilities: gym, tennis, swimming, sauna, steam-room, squash and bowling.

Al-Khozama   465 4650

Compound swimming pool

Hyatt Regency	479 1234
Marriott Hotel	477 9300
Minhal Holiday Inn	478 2500
Diplomatic Quarter	488 1010
FAL	454 3901

▸ *Hyatt Regency Hotel Sports Club* (T):
Facilities: swimming, sauna, gym, squash, jacuzzi, steam room
▸ *Marriott Hotel Sports Club* (T):
Facilities: sauna, steam-room, swimming, table-tennis, exercise room.
▸ *Minhal Holiday Inn* (T):
Facilities: gym, sauna, squash, swimming, massage
▸ *Diplomatic Quarter Sports Club* (T):
Within the Diplomatic Quarter is an extensive and beautifully-landscaped club which is open to families. Facilities: tennis, squash, football, karate, snooker, table-tennis, sauna and steam-room, gymnasium, indoor swimming and an outdoor pool with artificial waves (open in summer only, from May, and very popular with children). There are also well laid-out play areas for children. There are separate days for men and women to use the indoor and the outdoor pools.
▸ *FAL Sports Complex (T):*
This complex, on King Abdulaziz Sreet (Old Airport Road) at FAL shopping centre, offers the following to men and boys only: ice-skating, bowls, billiards,snooker, table-tennis, bar football and darts. All costs are per hour of play, ranging from SR25 for billiards to SR35 for ice skating. However, monthly and yearly memberships for ice skating are also available; these include free hire of skates and free use of the ice-skating rink.

Shisha There are also opportunities for men of all nationalities to meet over a coffee or hubble-bubble water pipe (*shisha*) to talk about business or any other subject in one of Riyadh's *shisha* parlours on the outskirts of town.

Golf

Inter-Continental Golf Course	465 5000 x 6146
Arizona Compound	248 3657 x 454
Dirab Golf & Recreation Centre	498 0018

Nine hole golf courses are available at the Inter-Continental Hotel (T), Arizona Compound (T) and the Dirab Golf & Recreation Centre (T); each has a pro shop with golf clubs, sports clothes and balls. Arizona and Dirab also have driving ranges and the Inter-Continental arranges group golf lessons for children during May, June, and July. Call the clubs for current information on memberships, competitions and schedules.

Football
There are a few club stadiums in Riyadh where men can go to watch football matches. The National Stadium, to the left of the Dammam Highway going east out of town, holds international matches from time to time. You can find out about these in the English-language newspapers.

Activities for children

There are a number of funfairs and play areas in Riyadh, some open to families, some to men or women only. Most of these

National Football Stadium

are open in the evenings and some are also open during the afternoons. (See also under Parks, page 73).

Diplomatic Quarter   There are beautifully landscaped play areas for children in the Diplomatic Quarter. They are open to all and often empty on weekdays. The Diplomatic Quarter Sports Club (*see* page 76) has a wave pool which is popular with children, and other sports facilities. Al-Manahil Center in the Diplomatic Quarter (*see* page 63) offers recreational and sports activities to children.

Janadriyah Road   If you take the road to Thumamah and Janadriyah (Route 550), going east from the Imam University (exit 8), the desert on both sides of the road is alive with activities for children. There are tracks for dune-buggy riding, pony trekking, horse riding and a 'luna park' funfair with an enormous slide. This is at its busiest on Thursday and Friday afternoons and evenings. Families are welcome here.

Reptile World (T), a display of live snakes, lizards, gekkos, skinks and chameleons, is on the top floor of al-Akariya Mall in Olaya. The poisonous snakes, including the native Black Snake, are clearly marked and are particularly fascinating. In the video room, visitors can learn how researchers "milk" the venom from poisonous snakes and how poison antidotes are made. Children, and brave adults can hold some of the non-poisonous snakes under supervision at the end of the tour.

Reptile World   493 3978

The Tent Park This is a permanent funfair run by and for women. Children love it: there are roller-coasters, big wheels, a ghost train and a little train which runs around the perimeter. It can amuse children aged from about two to twelve, and is extremely popular, particularly after dark when the atmosphere is at its most lively. Entrance costs SR3 per person and the rides are SR5 each. Don't buy the arm-band at SR35, as it does not entitle the wearer to go on all rides.

Playground in the Diplomatic Quarter

Opening times: 4.00-10.00 pm daily except Wednesdays and Thursdays, when it stays open until 11.00 pm.

Euromarché This supermarket has a funfair outside its front door. Men only.

Fast Food Restaurants All fast-food restaurants have rides for small children, for which you pay by inserting a coin. McDonald's also has free slides. This play equipment is open to families.

Ice-skating   454 3901

Ice Skating (T) is available for boys and men at the FAL Centre on Old Airport Road. An ice-skating league for boys has competed, in the past, with teams from Abu Dhabi and Kuwait as well as Germany. Ask at the Ice Skating Centre or around your compound for information.

Sports Teams such as roller blade hockey and swimming are active in Riyadh. Organised by parents on compounds these co-ed teams compete in a Riyadh league. The best swimmers go on to compete in a national championship. The compound teams welcome new enthusiasts and are often open to non-residents.

Riyadh Youth Athletic Association is another parent-organised unit which assigns students to area teams in basketball, soccer and softball according to the season. This group draws children from all schools and promotes friendly competition.

Motorcross A motorcross track has been built off the ring road. With races held on Friday mornings and fast food outlets in business, this area takes on a carnival like atmosphere with lots of excitement and fun. The races are graded by age. Bikes and go-karts are available for hire, as they are along the Janadriyah Road, but serious bikers may want to invest in a bike or dune buggy of their own. Excitement Dune Buggies (T) and Honda Cycles (T) on Olaya Road have a selection.

| Dune Buggies | 481 1473 |
| Honda Cycles | 464 6097 |

Organised tours in Riyadh

Willy D'Cunha, in association with the **Sahara Airport Hotel** (T), organises private tours with a personal guide to the old capital city of Dir'iyyah, Musmak Palace, and an overview of Riyadh. These are an excellent introduction to the area for business visitors or new residents. He also hosts group tours on Wednesdays, Thursdays and Fridays, with a minimum of ten people, for desert trips such as a fossil hunt or desert diamond search. On Sundays and Mondays a night-time tour of Riyadh, including a guided visit to the King Abdulaziz Historical Centre, ends with a dinner at the Panorama Restaurant in the Sahara Airport Hotel.

| Sahara Airport Hotel | 220 4500 |

Sightseekers (T) promotes overnight camping tours by camel in the desert areas outside Riyadh. In addition to riding a camel, clients can enjoy Bedouin dancing and singing, henna decoration of the hands, dinner under the stars, a search for desert diamonds, and some extraordinary scenery. Contact [Sightseekers@hotmail.com] or the Manager, Saad.

| Sightseekers | 055 469772 |

ACS (T) offers occasional bus tours of Riyadh, al-Faisaliyah Centre, and Dir'iyyah and also organises tours to other Middle Eastern countries and beyond.

| ACS | 482 9604 |

| Ambulance | 997 | Fire | 998 | Police | 999 |
| English speaking clock | 963 | Dir. Enquiries | 905 | Tel. Engineer | 904 |

List of telephone numbers referred to in text

A

ACS	482 9604
Adams	461 1853
ADEL	476 3510
al-Shola	478 2471
Cercon Building	464 5878
Malaaz	476 1543
Olaya Road	462 5882
Airport Information	220 2968
al-Ajami	464 3865
Al-Ajlan	465 8430
al-Ajlan Mens' Wear	465 8430
al Akariya Ladies Tailoring	465 8430
Alphagraphics	464 1600
Aman Veterinary Clinic	435 8661
Emergency cellular	055416 877
Beeper	115230603
American School	491 4270
Arab Motors	233 2222
Arabesque	482 3444 x 2705
Arizona Golf Course	248 3657 x 454
Armani	464 6537
Art Nouveau	416 2990
Arts & Antiques	464 8182
Ash-Sharq Distribution	479 1791
Assaraya Turkish Restaurant	464 9336
Attar Travel	478 7208
al-Azizia Supermarket	482 7055

B

Baalbek Rest.	462 1154
Badawia	464 3637
al-Bakar Real Estate	465 5006
al-Baljoon	404 1421
Bally	462 1587
al-Baker Real Estate	465 5006
Barakat Optical	476 9105
Bangkok Seafood Rest.	465 1416
al-Bateel	462 6019
Bayt al-Balloon	464 3996

Bazaar Assafarat	488 0627
Beautiful Gardens	464 0102
Beity	465 5449
Benetton	462 6871
Bin Gaith Establishment	465 5247
Birkenstock	462 7801
Bleu Marine	465 9560
Body Reform	463 0265
Body Shop	
al-Azizia	482 7904
Akariya, Olaya	463 3502
Bourj al-Hammam	
Aruba Street	465 7686
Takhasussii Street	441 1401
British Council	462 1818
Courses	480 7811
British School	248 2387
Al-Burj	462 0692

C

Café Can	465 8007
Camel Inc. Movers	454 6572
Carpet World	
Old Airport Rd)	478 6829
Olaya Rd	464 5419
Centre for Continuing Education -	
Women	402 4700
Men	402 8854
Centre Saoudien	476 6436
Les Châteaux	476 5559
Cheesecake Factory	488 3309
Chicco	462 4043
Chinatown	
al-Akariya	419 1263
al-Mousa	465 8021
Christian Dior	464 5696
Clarks	
al-Akariya Olaya	460 1308
al-Azizah Takhasussi	488 2593
Oruba Plaza	419 2521
Consulting Clinics	465 9100

Creators Maintenance	477 5863
Creators Real Estate	477 0249/478 6708

D

Dallah Hospital	454 5277
Dr Amal's Paediatric Clinic	476 0438/7425
Dr El Hayek	486 0459 x 34
Dr al-Humoud	465 6425
Da Pino	465 4650
Dar al-Angal	462 8197
Dar al-Uloum	477 7121/1952
Dawaliya	479 4507
Desert Rose	441 8748
Desert Swimming Pools	463 1696
Dewaish	479 4311
Dr Fatina al-Humoud	465 6425
DHL/SNAS	462 1919
Diplomat	465 2411
Diplomatic Quarter Sports Club	488 1010
Dirab Golf Course	498 0018
Dr. Maged el-Heyek	486 0459 x 34
	410 9354 x 34
cellular	055 208451
beeper	19442922
Dum Pukht	465 4109
Dune Buggies	481 1473
Dunia al-Beit	479 1322
Durrah Dive Centre	464 4134
Dutch School	275 0275

E

Early Learning Centre	
al-Azizia Takhasussi	480 3461
al-Nemer Centre	462 4695
Electrolux	419 2016
Elmark	465 1581
Euromarché supermarket.	482 5453
European Centre for Languages &	
Training	476 1218/4680/9698

F

FADS	456 0697
Faisal Saadawys	464 8182
al-Faisaliya Hotel	464 4650
FAL Sports Complex	454 3901/456 1889
Family Medical Clinic	465 5253

al-Faleh Sports Store	477 0505
Fauchon	462 7655
Fayfa	477 4761
FedEx	419 4220
Ferdaus Steakhouse	477 3900
Ferragamo	465 4322
Fitaihi	478 2012
Floriane/Kickers	464 8911
Food Basket	231 0113
Forsan	465 9144
Florsheim	
al-Akaria Sitteen	462 3124
al-Mousa Mall	478 9737
Fraihi Antiques	478 0965 x 22
French Connection	
French Corner	464 5322
French School	476 8501
Four Winds	454 4080
Funoon Accessories	419 0916
Furusato	465 7648

G

GAMA Dental Clinic	454 2929
GNC	463 3257
GNP	476 7597
GOSI Hospital	493 3000
Gazzaz	
al-Akaria Olaya	460 1801
Olaya Thalateen	462 6688
Sitteen	478 2668
Geneviève Lethu	464 1959
German School	456 7715
al-Ghadir Fashion	464 7663
Ghornatah Sports Shops	465 2064
Giafranco Ferre	465 8527
Gianni Versace	462 7493
Giorgio Armani	464 7060
Golden Dragon Rest.	462 7168
Good Ship Lollipop	462 4064
Ghornatah	465 2064
Green Crescent Health	464 4434
Guess	465 3754
Gulf Royal	463 1622/465 5368

H

Habitat	465 9877

Haagen Dazs	462 6241
Hakbani House	481 2068
Hala Limousines	
Sulaimaniya	463 3529
Akariya	465 1451
Eye Hospital	482 1234 x 1262
Hala Printing Press	482 9620
al-Hamadi Hospital	464 3312
Hasan Optical Centre	464 0630
House of Talents	465 9073
Home Plaza	462 5781
Hyatt Regency Hotel	479 1234

I

Iceskating	454 3901
ID Design	462 6159
IKEA	488 3233
Indian Embassy School	231 8092
Inter-Continental Hotel	465 5000
Golf Course	x 6146

J

Jacadi	478 4414
Jade Garden	465 0825
Jaeger	462 7059
Japanese School	241 2591
al-Jarir Bookshop, Olaya	462 6000
al-Jazeera Showtime	435 4633
Jazeerah spmkt.	465 5988
Jazirah Furnishing	463 2631
al-Jeraisy	462 3030
Sales	x 1181
Service	x 2817
Jotun Paints	446 8282

K

Kanoo Travel	477 2228
Kenzo	464 9317
Kickers/Floriane	464 8911
Kids' / Floriane	464 8911
Kids' Kingdom	463 4141
King Abdulaziz Public Library	491 1300
King Faisal Centre Museum	465 2255 x 6400
King Faisal Foundation Centre (fax)	465 9993
King Faisal Specialist Hospital	464 7272
King Fahad (National Guard)	
Hospital	252 0252

King Khalid Eye Specialist	
Hospital	482 1234
King Khalid Int. Airport	220 2968
Kingdom Dates	462 2444
al-Khozama Hotel	465 4650
al-Khozama Gourmet Shop	465 4650 x 654

L

La Sani	465 5666
Ladybird	461 1826
Lamsa	460 1214
Language Centre for Girls	464 9515
L'Ecluse	465 7648
Le Gourmet	
Olaya	465 4737
Sitteen St	476 3114
Lilac	462 9420
Liz Claiborne	462 4322

M

al-Madareb	465 7361
Mail Boxes Etc.	461 2047
al-Maktaba	
Malaz	476 1597
Olaya	464 4064
al-Manahil Centre	482 9755
al-Manhal Water	498 4883
Marhaba Rest.	462 2070
al-Marikh	464 7531/465 8523
Marriott Hotel	477 9300
al-Marsam	464 4374
MAX	235 3650
Memories of China	462 6609
MEPPS	465 0951
Mees Mees Cottons	462 6030
Memory Lane	462 5666 x 1207
Mexican Connection	450 9575
Mexx	461 5934
Middle East Centre for Human	
Development	465 1505
Military Hospital (RKH)	477 7714
Minhal Holiday Inn	478 2500
al-Mishari Hospital	464 7700
al-Moghreby	488 6156
al-Moghtara Farm	462 8363
al-Mourouj Postal Service	460 1161

Mothercare	465 1803
al-Multaka	478 3388
Multinational School	454 1686
Museum of Archaeology and	
Ethnography	402 5093
Musicmaster	465 5190
al-Mutlaq Furniture	465 1835
al-Mutlaq Novotel	476 0000

N

al-Nahda Philanthropic Society	464 9259
al-Nahda Special Rehabilitation	
Centre Shop	478 2583/2474
al-Nakheel Rest	465 4650
Namma Cargo Services	465 4200
Naseej	080 124 1333
National Commission of Wildlife	
(NCWCD) tel: 441 0369; fax: 441 0797	
National Museum	402 9500 x 1082
National Veterinary Clinic	40303 3494
Nawras Nest	
Old Airport Rd	478 1881
Olaya Rd	465 6222
Nejd Village	464 6540
Neuhaus Choc.	462 1555
Next	461 4973
Le Nôtre	466 1465

O

Oasis	464 2512
Obal	463 4476
Obeikan	465 0129
Occasions	464 1545
Okarina	465 6622
al-Ola Real Estate	465 9704
Olaya Holiday Inn	461 2000
Orbit	479 3464
Oriental Carpet Bazaar	477 7782
Oriental Supermarket	463 4076

P

Panda supermarket	
Aruba	465 322
Olaya	464 4992
Panorama Restaurant	220 4500
Patchi	465 9768

Picnic Stop	450 0088
Pizza Hut (delivery)	463 1303
Planters	465 9986
Port Store	463 3169
Pottery Plus	461 3213
Prenatal	463 4315
Prima Donna	462 4995
Primenet	460 1972
ProGolf	479 3872
Puma	465 0477

Q

Q-zar	463 2531

R

Radio Riyadh	403 8111
Rahm Dental & Implant Service	488 4084
Red Sea Divers	450 0365
Reptile World	493 3978
Riyadh Vet. Clinic	456 6376/456 6376
Emergency cellular	055 644 648
Riyadh Palace Hotel	405 4444
Roma Restaurant	464 1133
Rosa	
headquarters	463 4023
by SACO	464 1203
Ruby Jewellers	476 6443

S

SACO Hardware	
FAL	464 6700
Rawda	233 2463
Takhassusi	482 9230
SAMES Pest Control	476 9989
SARA	463 2693
Sa'ad al-Rasheed Services Corp.	403 0900
Safari Travel	477 2525
Safeways - see Tamimi	
Sahara Airport Hotel	220 4500
al-Saleh Eye Care	478 6660
Salvatore Ferragamo	465 6538
Samir Photo.	465 1453
Samha Printing Press	465 8976
Sarawat Supermarket	464 6856/6847
Saudi Fisheries	462 4741
Saudi House	465 3515

Saudi Limousines	463 1416	Thimar	477 7690
Sawani	441 7106	Thumamah Research Cent.	482 9604
Saysan Ladies Tailoring	465 5481	Tihama	401 2969
Science Oasis	482 8276	Tiffany & Tomato	465 3432
Sea & Sun	479 2550	Tihama Books	401 2969
Seven Four Seven	463 2291	Toyland	464 8312
Shaabiyah	419 8581	Toys R Us	419 5555
Shamsan Photos	463 1476	Tokyo Rest.	464 5672
Shamsan Stores	465 3957	Transad Clinic	465 0840
Sharquia Art Supplies	488 0872	True Value	476 9099
Shary Limousines	477 7313	Tutti Naturale	465 1755
Shathly Electronics	464 6911		
al-Shegrey Bookstore	462 8684	**U**	
Sheraton Hotel	454 3300	UPS	800 124 6699/482 6655
Shezan Rest.	462 6608		
Shoe Mart	419 2097	**V**	
Shoe Palace	643 0121	Versace	462 7493
Shogun	479 1234	Video Channel 3	465 1955
Sightseekers	055469772	The Village	463 4211
Silk Roads	472 1620		
Specialised Medical Centre	416 4000	**W**	
Spine & Sports Injury Clinic	480 2360	Wajbah Rest.	453 1086
Splash	419 6836	Wardeh	463 0731
Sports Kingdom	462 4601	al-Watania Organic	496 1749
Steak House, Olaya	464 9638	Western Cowboy	419 1259
Sultan Garden Cent.	465 5555 ext 275	Wheels	464 3321
Swedish School	246 2400 x 2465		
		Y	
T		Yamal Asham	461 3293
Tables and Traditions	462 3487		
Tamimi Markets (Safeways)	453 1472	**Z**	
FAL	463 3973	Z	464 8911
King Fahad Rd	453 1472	Zaina/Sears	477 2155
al-Tayyar Travel Cent.	463 3133	Zajil	462 1756

Airline Offices

Zamani Framers   461 6225
Unless otherwise indicated , these are located in one of the following:

(1) **Kanoo Tower** – behind the Minhal Holiday Inn.
(2) **ACE Travel** – American Express Building, on Dammam/Makkah Highway between King Abdulaziz Street (Old Airport Road) and Olaya Road.
(3) **King Faisal Foundation building** – behind the al-Khozama Hotel, between Olaya Road and King Fahad Highway.
(4) **King Abdulaziz Street** (Old Airport Road) – opposite Minhal Hotel.
(5) **Circon Building** – opposite al-Akariya shopping centre, just off Olaya Road.
(6) **Attar Travel** – behind the Pepsi Cola Building.

Air Algérie	465 5885 *(3)*
Air Canada	477 2228 x 288*(1)*
	Air France:
Sales/Reservations	476 9666 *(4)*
Air India	477 4484 x 291/2 *(1)*
Air Lanka	478 8935 x 291/2 *(1)*
Air New Zeland	479 3930 *(6)*
Alitalia	461 6008
American Airlines	462 2367 *(3)*
Austrian Airlines:	478 7208 *(6)*
Bimam: Bangladesh Airlines	462 3376 *(2)*
British Airways:	
Sales/Reservations	800 244 4777 *(3)*
Cathay Pacific	479 3232
Dammam Road, by Gulf Bridge	
Cyprus Air	478 7212 *(6)*
Delta Airlines	461 3688 *(2)*
Emirates.Airlines	465 7117 *(5)*
Ethiopian Airlines	478 2140/9763 *(4)*
Garuda Indonesia	465 2978 *(5)*
Gulf Air: *Olaya Road*	

Sales	464 4090
Reservations	462 6666
Supervisor Reservations	464 4220
Japan Airlines	464 5056
Olaya Road	
KLM	477 4777 x 206/7/9 *(1)*
Korean Airways	465 2949 *(3)*
Kuwait Airlines	463 1218 *(3)*
Lufthansa: Sales	463 2680 *(3)*
Reservations	463 2004
Malaysian Airlines	476 4085 *(4)*
Middle East Airlines	465 6600*(4)*
(MEA)	465 8468
Northwest Airlines	462 5046*(3)*
	Olympic:
Sales/Reservations	464 4596
Khozama Centre - first floor	
Philippine Airlines	478 0336 *(1)*
PIA	465 9600
Between Dabbab St. & Olaya Rd.	
Qantas	477 2228 x 289/305 *(1)*
Royal Jordanian (ALIA) Airlines	462 5697
On Olaya Thalateen	
Saudia: Reservations	488 5555/4444
Sales no phone	
King Fahad Highway, behind al-Owais market	
Flight Information	222 111
Scandinavian Airlines	479 3930 *(6)*
Singapore Airlines	465 6791 *(5)*
Swissair: Sales	477 5429 *(4)*
Reservations	476 6444
Syrian Arab Airlines	465 4231*(3)*
Thai Airlines	476 6776*(4)*
Turkish Airlines	463 1600
Olaya Rd.	
TWA	477 8666
Old Akariya, Sitteen	
United Airlines	477 2228 x 290/304*(1)*
Yemenia	403 9248
Khazzan St.close to Masjid Johara	

Compounds

ABV ROC	403 7878
al-Hamra Oasis Village	249 0440
al-Mustaqbal Homes	465 7177
al-Reem	454 1028
al-Romaizan	410 9106
al-Salam Villas	456 9662
al-Wadi/Waha	488 7611
al-Waha Gardens Village	410 4265
Arab Investment	482 3444
Arabian Homes	454 1888
Arizona	248 4444
ASASCO Compound	419 0936
ASASCO Village	463 1014
AT&T	482 7017/241 1055
Ballast Needham	232 6090
Boeing B-2	482 6672
Boeing O-3	492 0508
Boeing 60 Villa	465 0057
COLSA	248 3475
Cordoba	248 3471
Dywidag	246 4144
Eid	248 2580/3366
FAL	248 5847
JECOR	464 0433
Jeddawal	249 9500
King Faisal Hospital Housing	252 0252
Kingdom City	275 0275
Lockheed	2410919
Mirage	488 6999
Najd	248 1040
al-Nakheel	248 3090
Namma	465 4200
OPM Sang	464 6156
Palms	482 9093
Palms Villas (KFS Hosp.)	464 7272
Philips Ericsson (Riyadh Village)	246 2400
Phillip Holtzman	241 2479
Phoenix	2302755
Rhoda	231 0754
ROC	241 2800
Sahara Towers	462 5666
SAIS-R Teachers	493 1741

Saudi British Bank	464 2306/463 1363
Shabib Village	488 7191
Star	488 1404
USMTM	478 1100
Villa Rosas	488 7611
Vinnell	246 3200
al-Yamama	241 3267

National Groups and Embassies

American Community Services (ACS)	482 9604

This organisation is open to Americans and non-Americans and has a wonderful range of activities on offer - a must for all newcomers.

Afghanistan	480 3459
Albania	456 9396
Algeria	488 7171
Argentina	465 2600
Australia	488 7788
Austria	480 1217
Bangladesh	465 5300
Belgium	488 2888
Bosnia	456 7914
Brazil	488 0018
Brunei	456 0814
Burkino Faso	465 2224
Burundi	464 1155
Cameroon	488 0022
Canada	488 2288
Chad	465 7702
Czechoslovakia	450 3617
Denmark	488 0101
Egypt	465 8425
Finland	488 1515
France	488 1255
Gabon	456 7173
Gambia	463 4532
Germany	488 0700

Ghana	464 2766	Oman	482 3120
Greece	465 1974	Pakistan	488 7272
Guinea	231 0631	Palestine	488 0744
Hungary	454 6707	People's Republic of China	462 4246
		Philippines	488 0835
India	488 4144	Poland	454 9274
Indonesia	488 2800	Portugal	462 2115
Iran	488 1916		
Ireland	488 2300	Qatar	482 5544
Italy	488 1212	Romania	456 6205
		Rwanda	470 4545
Japan	488 1100	Senegal	454 2144
Jordan	488 0039	Singapore	465 7007
		Somalia	463 2774
Kazakhstan	470 1839	South Africa	454 3723
Kenya	488 2484	Spain	488 0606
Korea	488 2211	Sri Lanka	454 1745
Kuwait	488 3500	Sudan	488 7979
		Sweden	488 3100
Lebanon	465 1000	Switzerland	488 1291
Liberia	450 3602		
Libya	454 4511	Taiwan	488 1900
		Tanzania	454 2839
Malaysia	488 7100	Thailand	488 1174
Mali	419 5640	Tunisia	488 7900
Malta	463 2345	Turkey	482 0101
Mauritania	465 6313		
Mexico	482 8218	Uganda	454 4910
Morocco	482 6382	United Arab Emirates	482 9652
		United Kingdom	488 0077
Nepal	403 6433	United States	488 3800 x1536 (CLO)
Netherlands	488 0011	Uruguay	462 0739
New Zealand	488 7988		
Niger	464 2931	Venezuela	476 7867
Nigeria	482 3024		
Norway	488 1904	Yemen	488 1769

Additional reading

Cathy Cuddihy: *Saudi Customs and Etiquette* (Peregrine Publishing)
William Facey: *Riyadh – The Old City* (Immel Publishing)
William Facey: *Dir'iyyah and the First Saudi State* (Stacey International)
James Peters: *Very Simple Arabic* (Stacey International)
James Peters: *The Arab World Handbook* (Stacey International)
Sir Donald Hawley: *Courtesies in the Gulf* (Stacey International)
Ionis Thompson: *Desert Treks from Riyadh* (Stacey International)
Jim Stabler: *The Desert Driver's Manual* (Stacey International)

Maps

The following maps are much simplified approximations of Riyadh's road system, to help readers identify places referred to in the book. For more accurate and wide-ranging information, consult Zaki Farsi's *City Map and Guide to Riyadh*, which can be bought at any good bookshop. While names, e.g. Turki, have been standardised for the purpose of these maps, they sometimes vary in transliteration on public signs.

Popular names for some streets and places survive long after the original reason for the name has disappeared, which can be confusing for the new-comer. For example:

Coffee-pot roundabout, the circle (roundabout) in front of the RSAF air-base (the old airport) is so named for the sculpture which used to stand on the site of the fountain.

Everything Street, Thalateen Olaya Street, is so called because a shop selling 'everything' used to stand on this street.

Sang Road, Thalateen Olaya Street is sometimes called this for the OPM Sang compound which stands there.

Circle Supermarket Street, Thalateen Sulaimaniya Street.

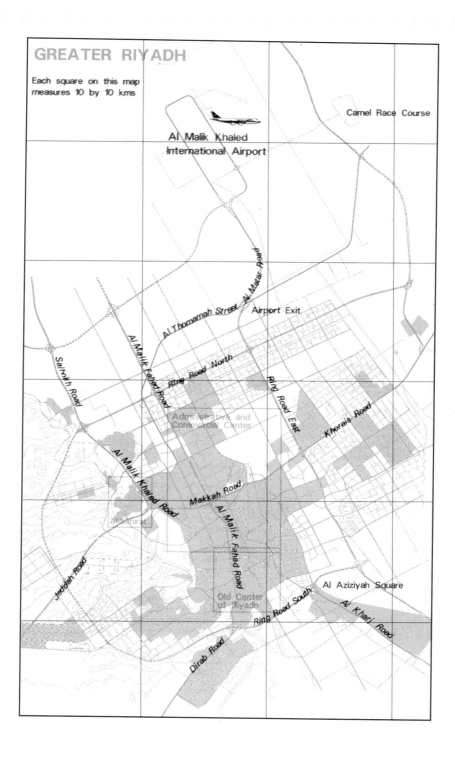

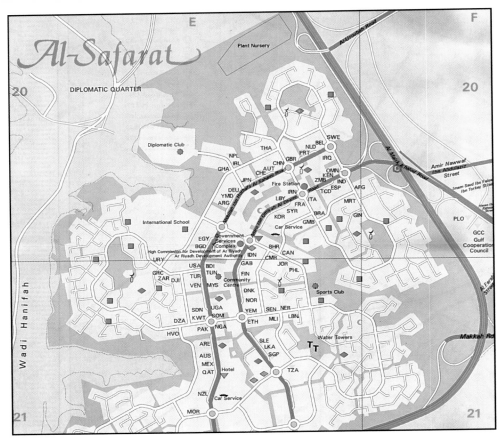

CODE	EMBASSY	ESP	Spain	KWT	Kuwait	SDN	Sudan
		ETH	Ethiopia	LBN	Lebanon	SEN	Senegal
AFG	Afghanistan	FIN	Finland	LBY	Libya	SGP	Singapore
ARE	United Arab Emirates	FRA	France	LKA	Sri Lanka	SLE	Sierra Leone
ARG	Argentina	GAB	Gabon	MOR	Morocco	SOM	Somalia
AUS	Australia	GBR	Great Britain	MEX	Mexico	SWE	Sweden
AUT	Austria	GHA	Ghana	MLI	Mali	SYR	Syria
BDI	Burundi	GIN	Guinea	MRT	Mauretania	TCD	Tchad
BEL	Belgium	GMB	Gambia	MYS	Malaysia	THA	Thailand
BGD	Bangladesh	GRC	Greece	NER	Niger	TUN	Tunisia
BHR	Bahrain	HVO	Bourkina	NGA	Nigeria	TUR	Turkey
BRA	Brazil	IDN	Indonesia	NLD	The Netherlands	TZA	Tanzania
CAN	Canada	IND	India	NOR	Norway	UGA	Uganda
CHE	Switzerland	IRL	Ireland	NPL	Nepal	URY	Uruguay
CHN	China	IRN	Iran	NZL	New Zealand	USA	United States
CMR	Cameroon	IRQ	Iraq	OMN	Oman	VEN	Venezuela
DEU	Germany	ITA	Italy	PAK	Pakistan	YEM	Yemen, Arab.rep.
DJI	Djibouti	JOR	Jordan	PHL	Philippines	YMD	Yemen, Peoples rep.
DNK	Denmark	JPN	Japan	PLO	PLO	ZAR	Zaire
DZA	Algeria	KEN	Kenya	PRT	Portugal	ZMB	Zambia
EGY	Egypt	KOR	Korea	QAT	Qatar		

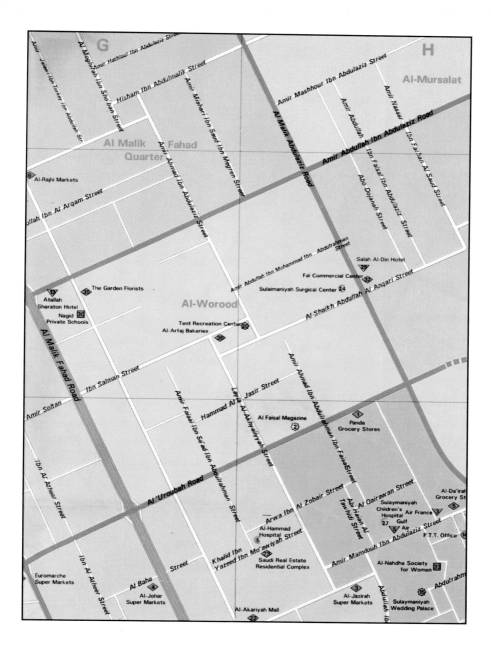

Amir Jaber Ibn Torkey Ibn Abdullah Str

Amir Moghirah Ibn Sho'ban Street

G

Hisham Ibn Abdulmalik Street

Amir Hathlout Ibn Abdulaziz Stre

Amir Misheri Ibn Saud Ibn Megren Street

Amir Ahmad Ibn Abdulaziz Street

Al Malik Fahad
Quarter

Amir Mashhour Ibn Abdulaziz Street

Al-Mursalat

H

Al Malik Abdulaziz Road

Amir Abdullah Ibn Abdulaziz Road

Amir Abdullah Ibn Faisal Ibn Abdulaziz Street

Amir Nasser

Ibn Farhan Al Saud Street

Abo Dojanah Street

Al-Rajhi Markets

uillah Ibn Al Arqam Street

The Garden Florists

Atallah
Sheraton Hotel

Nagid
Private Schools

Al-Worood

Amir Abdullah Ibn Mohammad Ibn Abdulrahman Street

Salah Al-Din Hotel

Fal Commercial Center

Sulaimaniyah Surgical Center 24

Al-Shaikh Abdullah Al Angari Street

Tent Recreation Center

Al-Arfaj Bakeries

Ibn Salman Street

Amir Soltan

Al Malik Fahad Road

Amir Faisal Ibn Sa'ad Ibn Abdulrahman Street

Hammad Al Jasir Street

Layla Al-Akhyaliyyah Street

Amir Ahmad Ibn Abdulrahman Ibn Faisal Street

Al Faisal Magazine

Panda
Grocery Stores

Al 'Uroubah Road

Ibn Al Atheer Street

Arwa Ibn Al Zobair Street

Abi Hanan Al Tawhidi Street

Al Dairawan Street

Sulaymaniyah
Children's
Hospital Air France

Gulf

Al-Da'irah
Grocery St

27

Air

Al-Hammad
Hospital

Khalid Ibn
Yazeed Ibn Mo'awiyah Street

Street

Saudi Real Estate
Residential Complex

Amir Mamdouh Ibn Abdulaziz Street

P.T.T. Office

Al-Nahdha Society
for Women

Abdulrahm

Euromarche
Super Markets

Ibn Al Atheer Street

Al Baha

Al-Johar
Super Markets

Al-Jazirah
Super Markets

Sulaymaniyah
Wedding Palace

Abdullah Ibn

Al-Akariyah Mall

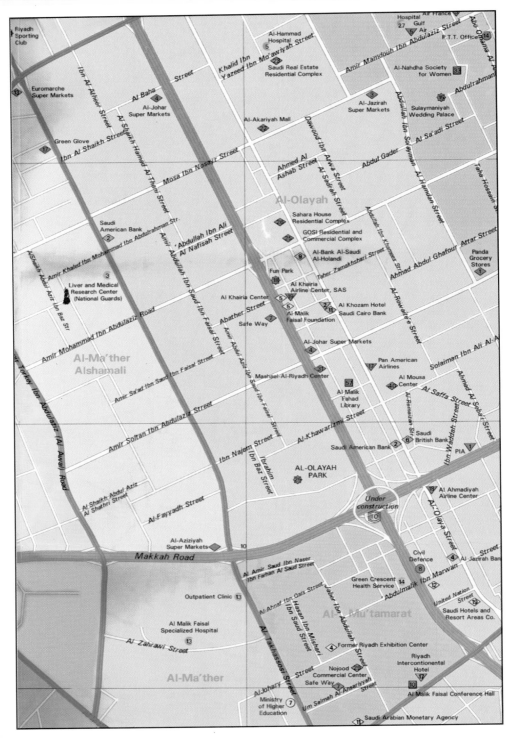

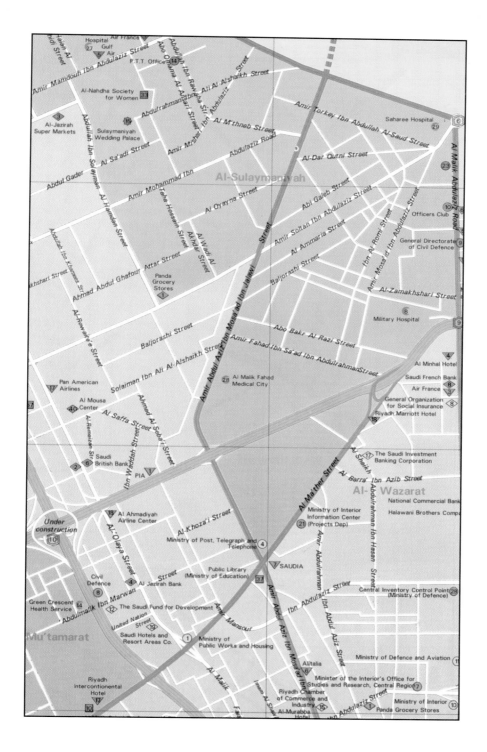

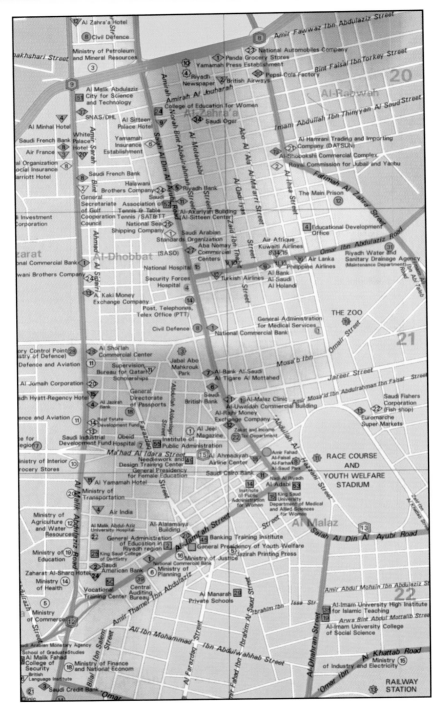

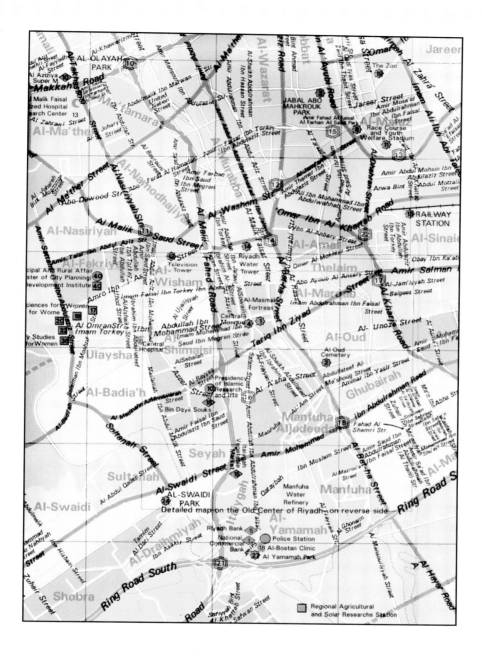

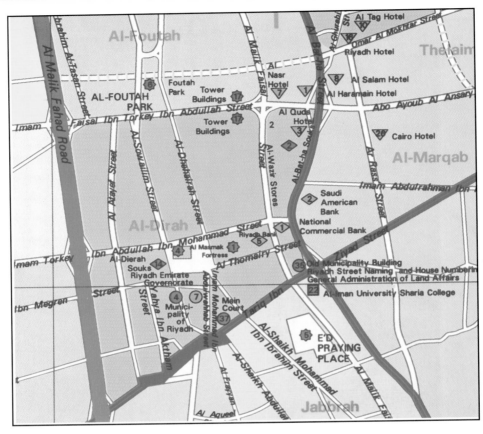